THE CONSTRUCTION OF
model open boats

Overleaf: *The frontispiece is the Author's demonstration model of the various stages of his technique for modelling open boats. (Photograph by courtesy of John Bowen)*

A METHOD OF MODEL OPEN BOAT CONSTRUCTION

Stage 1. Two blocks of lime and keel plate. Note (a) direction of annular rings in blocks and (b) keel plate in quarter sawn.

Stage 2. Blocks and keel plate roughly sawn to shape.

Stage 3. Outside of blocks shaped to body lines and profile. Keel plate partly finished to size.

Stage 4. Blocks hollowed out to thickness in scale. Keel plate finished to shape and size.

Stage 5. Shell glued up. Note dowels giving correct register. Hog glued in. N.B. if for a carvel hull, fitting out can now begin.

Stage 6. Inside completely, outside partly planked. Transom glued on. Note (a) marks of run of planks (b) cut from bristol board.

Stage 7. Planking completed. Gunwales glued in. Timbers of apple wood sprung in. Thwart clamps and thwarts fitted. Bottom boards fixed.

Stage 8. Fitting out completed. Rudder hung. Mast stepped and rigged. Finished boat painted in suitable colours.

THE CONSTRUCTION OF

model open boats

by Ewart C. Freeston

MODEL SHIPWRIGHT
GREENWICH

© 1975 Model Shipwright

Published by
Conway Maritime Press Limited
7 Nelson Road, Greenwich, London SE10
ISBN 0 85177 080 0

Set by Jaset
Printed by Page Bros (Norwich) Ltd

Foreword

Probably every proud captain in the Navy or Merchant Service has, at some time or another, called the vessel which he commanded his boat. Only a pedant would object to his doing so. But for the purposes of this book it is necessary to define our terms and say exactly what is a boat. Fincham in 1812 says, 'Boats are small open vessels named according to the purpose for which they are intended; they are impelled by oars or sails.' to which now-a-days we can add 'or motors'.

The essential feature of a boat is that it is undecked or at most only partially decked; that it is small, certainly no larger than about 50'0" long; and that it can be called a launch, barge, cutter, gig, wherry, or some other name. It can be smooth sided, called carvel built; or with planks that overlap each other, called clinker built.

Being small they can be modelled at a large scale of say, 1/12 and made in exactly the same way as a real boat is built; but if they are to be modelled at a small scale and shown as boats stowed on the deck of a ship of the line or a tea clipper, or perhaps as an example of an inshore fishing boat and mounted in a glass case as a specimen of the modelmaker's art, then a different technique has to be adopted, and that is what this book is about.

It describes a way to make realistic models of boats, of either carvel or clinker build, which is adaptable to naval boats, fishing boats or pleasure boats. The fact is that so numerous are the examples of boats, in this country alone, that a lifetime of modelmaking devoted to one of these classes would not exhaust the subjects. Skill, determination and aptitude are necessary but, as a long term and worth-while project, this has much to recommend it. Unfortunately, so many of the everyday maritime features of the world are becoming rapidly things of the past, and their only existence being in people's memories.

                        Herstmonceux   **Ewart C Freeston**

ACKNOWLEDGEMENTS

The publishers would like to thank the following for their help in the production of this book:
Basil Bathe and Joe Roome of the Science Museum, London; John L Bowen; Gray Art Gallery and Museum, Hartlepool; Great Yarmouth Museums; Doughty Museum, Grimsby; Hull Maritime Museum; D Lester King and the Port of Lowestoft Research Society; David Lyon of the National Maritime Museum, Greenwich; Sunderland Museum; Martin Treadway; Whitby Museum; E N Wilson.

Contents

Introduction	*page* 8
Construction	11
Chapter 1 Making the shell	13
Chapter 2 Planking the shell	23
Chapter 3 Fitting out and displaying the model	29
Representative open boats	35
Chapter 4 Aldeburgh boats	36
Chapter 5 Lowestoft shrimping boats	44
Chapter 6 Cobles	48
Chapter 7 Sheringham crabbing boats	61
Chapter 8 Peter boats	66
Chapter 9 Thames wherries	76
Chapter 10 Southwold beach yawls	84
Appendices	91
Glossary	92
Further research	94

Introduction

Of any type of vessel, that of the open boat is probably the most numerous. It does not matter whether one considers liners, oil tankers, freight carriers, pleasure steamers, naval fighting ships or any other class of ship. Wherever there is sufficient water to float them, open boats can be found; on rivers, creeks, estuaries, ponds, lakes, beaches and also on the larger vessels already named in the form of lifeboats, workboats or tenders. Yet to find a really good model of one of them is the exception rather than the rule.

It is difficult to give an adequate reason for this. Though there are many excellent—one might even concede perfect—models of larger ships of every sort in museums or private hands in the case of open boats one has to search far and wide to find a passably good one; an excellent one is rarer, and a perfect one exceptional.

To the average ship modelmaker it may seem that a small open boat is both insignificant and unimportant, but this should not be so. From these craft the development of all ships has stemmed, starting with the dug-out canoe, to the built-up boat, to the oared galley with sails, and thence to the larger vessels of modern times as knowledge and techniques of shipbuilding have improved. All are basically developments of the open boat.

Another possible reason for the lack of good models is that though it looks easy to build one, in actual fact it requires not only a knowledge of how boats are built, but also a different approach and technique from that used in building a model of, say, a large cargo boat, destroyer or sailing ship. It also requires a degree of skill, a matter which will quickly become apparent once a start is made.

If one studies most large models and looks carefully for the boats stowed on deck, one will discover that often they are nothing more than shaped blocks of wood conveniently covered with a piece of material to represent canvas; and in so doing the maker has deceived no one but himself. It is quite apparent that he has taken an easy way out of what he thought was an unimportant part of the model and tacitly admitted his ignorance and the inadequacy of his skill by using a solid block of wood to represent a shell. If he has attempted to hollow out the block, it is often grossly out of scale and not of correct form. If he has gone a stage further and added timbers, these are usually of incorrect scantling, few in number and clearly unable to support the sides of the hull. The thwarts may be there, but rarely the knees, thwart clamps, stringers and other small but essential parts of the structure. If he has attempted to build a clinker hull, often it has less than the proper number of strakes, the run of the planking is hardly ever like the real thing, and shows the builder not only had little idea of how a boat is built, but has failed to study in detail the numerous examples of the real thing to be seen virtually on his own doorstep.

The boat in the first photograph illustrates some of these points; the timbers appear to be about 1′6″ apart (instead of the more usual 6″ to 1′0″) and they, and the thwarts, are badly over scale size. There are only six strakes, of which the garboard appears to be badly fitted. No provision has been made for rowlocks or thole pins.

Look now at the photograph of a 28′0″ whaleboat under construction, which I made to a scale of 1/4″ = 1′0″ and compare it with the model. Further comment might be unnecessary except to say that this shows the real thing in miniature, true to scale and with every detail shown. The timbers

Top: A commercial 'clinker' dinghy about 5½″ long. Below: The Author's 28′ New Bedford whaleboat under construction. The scale is 1/4″ = 1′0″. (Photographs by courtesy of the Author)

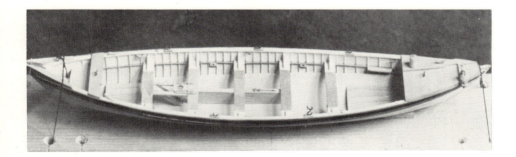

are correctly spaced, the thwarts have clamps and knees, the mast supports are fitted, and the bottom boards and foot walings are in place around the centre board and trunk. All the other fittings are included which gives the whole an air of reality.

In a model of a large ship much can be faked (if you will pardon the expression) without detracting from a good appearance. For instance, the hull can be a solid core planked over; deck houses can be solid blocks with dummy doors; it is not absolutely necessary for decks to be supported by scale size beams, carlins, knees and so on. Yet any of these examples, or others that can be thought of, cannot really condemn an otherwise splendid model. Only the purist might take exception to it. There are, so I am reliably informed, some models in which everything is built up as in the real ship, but the interior and the work of the maker remains invisible unless the model is taken to pieces.

In building an open boat true to scale, with every fitting shown, one can see at once if any part has been omitted. Even in those with half decks nothing is hidden; it is all clearly visible. One can see right up into the bows, through the bottom boards, below the thwarts, and everywhere one looks, inside or outside, all is manifest. It follows then that a certain degree of skill is required to achieve a first class result; this can only be acquired by practice, Given an ability to work accurately and with precision in wood, metal and card, together with the determination to work carefully and unhurriedly, one will be able to produce a perfect scale model of an open boat.

Construction

The Author's model of the Southwold beach yawl. (Photograph by courtesy of John Bowen)

CHAPTER 1

Making the shell

The first necessity for a good model, it goes without saying, is a good drawing. But this is not an unnecessary statement, for in addition to a good drawing one also requires a complete specification of the details. This is not impossible to acquire because many of the official draughts of naval boats, which can be obtained from the National Maritime Museum reproduced to a number of common scales, have all these details appended to the drawings. However, if one cannot obtain the specification, one can make an intelligent estimate of the missing details by comparison with a boat of similar type and date, and it is doubtful if one would be very far, if at all, in error.

In the case of inshore fishing boats or river craft we are faced with a different problem because many of these were never built from a drawing but on moulds made by the boatbuilder, and fashioned, by eye or rule of thumb, by men whose skill and learning passed from father to son and the details of which were never committed to paper. The lines of some of these local craft have been taken off by interested persons and can be found in many museums, notably the Science Museum, London and the National Maritime Museum, Greenwich, London, SE10.

The last resort of course, if one finds an example of the right prototype, is to take off the lines oneself, to measure it up, prepare a set of drawings, and so with the aid of photographs put on record types of craft which are disappearing (all too quickly) from our coasts, as for example, local fishing boats of the East Coast and Scottish fishing villages, or the clinker built rowing boats and punts of our rivers and lakes.

For the purposes of this book, I am taking as a basic example, a Gravesend Waterman's Wherry of about 1920.

This is a clinker built, transom-ended boat of 20'6" in length, and was the

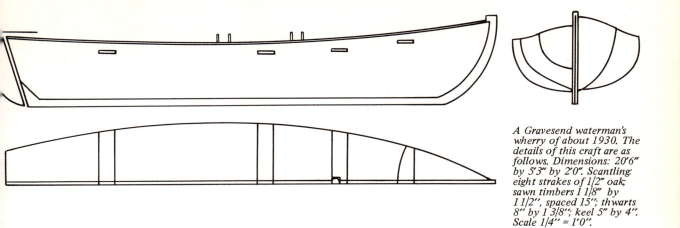

A Gravesend waterman's wherry of about 1930. The details of this craft are as follows. Dimensions: 20'6" by 5'3" by 2'0". Scantling: eight strakes of 1/2" oak; sawn timbers 1 1/8" by 1 1/2", spaced 15"; thwarts 8" by 1 3/8"; keel 5" by 4". Scale 1/4" = 1'0".

sort of boat used by watermen on the Thames to ferry passengers and goods from ship to shore, or as craft to be hired for short journeys up and down river. I shall show how to make a model of this to a scale of 1/4" = 1'0", but will add from time to time details for other types not relevant to this boat, though fundamentally once one has learnt how to construct this model other types are not really very much at variance with it.

I feel it is appropriate, before going further, to give a general outline of my method of the construction of model open boats, so that the reader will have a picture of the process as a consecutive whole before I go into details. The technique is to build up the boat as a thin shell, which is made by hollowing out, by a special process, two half blocks of wood, and then glueing them together each side of a central keel plate. Thus one can build a carvel boat true to scale. If the boat is clench built the shell is planked over inside and outside with scale thickness planks. When the shell has been completed the timbers, bottom boards, stringers, thwarts and all the other fittings are added and finally the boat is painted. During the construction, to make sure all parts fit together accurately, a number of templates are required, and these will be described as the process is outlined.

I consider that this method of construction is a great improvement on existing methods; indeed I will go further and say, quite categorically, that it is the best method of all, producing results far superior to any others hitherto seen. If the model is made from a solid block of wood one will be unable to reduce it to scale thickness, but even if it is thinned as far as skill allows, the shell will be unbalanced because of the inherent nature of the material itself. It will twist and distort as conditions vary; but with my method the wood is cut in a special way so as to balance the stresses set up, and it gives a shell which will remain stable, even though unpainted, until the timber

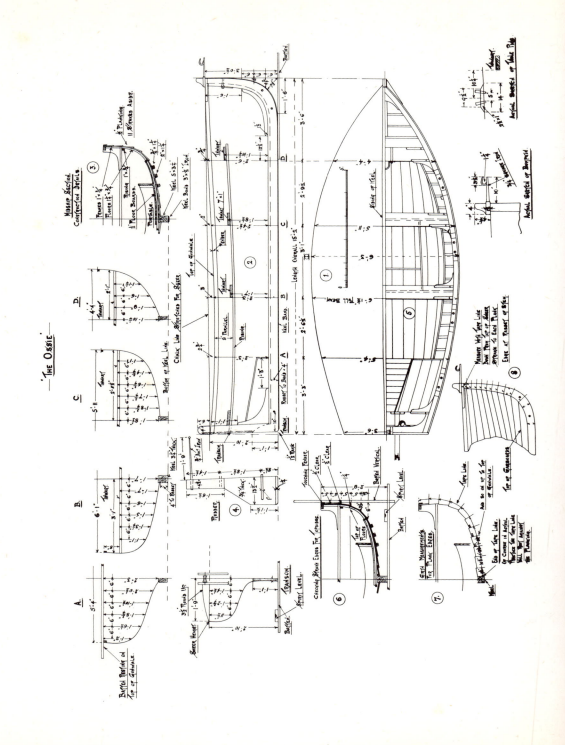

itself disintegrates. If the model is made on a mould that will be removed subsequently to allow the addition of timbers, thwarts and so forth, the removal of this mould will leave the shell unsupported. Thus, with the addition of each interior fitting, the structure will be weakened further, so that even a strong shell will become an unstable and fragile construction which must eventually collapse. With my method one begins with a thin shell which is delicate and fragile, but with every timber added, and as each thwart is fixed, the structure becomes firmer, giving an amazingly strong whole which when completed is almost unbreakable, and which will last for generations without sign of collapse or distortion.

The next question is one of the best wood to use for the model. For this I have only one answer: lime. It is the ideal wood for this method and I have found no other that is even nearly as good. It is a sweet cutting wood, hard but easy to carve with sharp tools; it will glue readily and accept paint beautifully. But above all, it is stable and if well seasoned will never distort even when reduced to extremely thin sections. It has no pronounced grain and therefore has no hard and soft parts to induce an uneven surface. For the timbers, thwart clamps and stringers apple wood is preferable because it can be sawn to very small sections without fear of collapse, and can be bent into sharp curves satisfactorily. However, lime will make a good substitute. For a coloured wood to be used to represent mahogany backboards or benches, pear wood is just right, but again lime can be used without introducing an objectionable appearance.

So now we are ready to start by procuring (A) a piece of lime a little larger all round than the boat will be, or else (B) a piece of half the width but twice the length. Whichever piece is chosen, it must be planed up with a sharp, finely set plane so that the sides are exactly square to the faces; and to save repeating myself I must insist that at all stages one must be prepared to work to precise and accurate measurements.

If one now looks at the end grain of the piece of wood the annular or growth rings show as arcs of circles.

In the case of piece (A) saw it in half lengthwise and reverse one piece end to end, or in the case of piece (B) saw it in half crosswise and turn one piece back on itself. If one now looks at the end grain the growth rings show up in the form of curved Vs or Us corresponding to the shape of the section of a hull.

Opposite page: A diagram showing how to take off the lines of a small boat, in this case the Aldeburgh boat 'Ossie'. (By courtesy of the Science Museum, London)

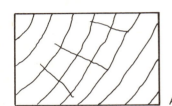 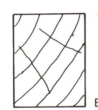 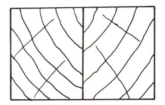

Both A and B are possible starting shapes, but both will look like the figure nearest left when sawn and planed properly.

The grain of the keel piece.

Since the strongest part of a tree is along the lines of the growth rings, it is easy to see that the natural strength of the wood is being used to form the boat and at the same time balancing one side against the other and thus eliminating any stresses. Check up on the planed surfaces (one of the sawn faces of piece (A) will have to be re-planed to match its neighbour) to see that the adjoining faces are in perfect contact.

The next piece of wood required is for the keel plate, and this should be large enough to include the stem and stern post. It must be sawn on the full quarter; that is, so that the growth rings are at right angles to the face, and then planed to scale thickness.

This is the first stage and the quality of the finished model depends upon the accuracy of the work so far.

These three pieces can now be laid aside while preparing the first pair of templates. These are made of any suitable flat sheet metal; I use brass, but any other fairly stout gauge metal will serve. One template (C) is cut and filed to the shape of the half-breadth plan but excluding the thickness of the keel. The second template (D) is cut and filed to the shape of the profile, excluding the keel: that is, to the line representing the top of the gunwale and the bearding line on the stem, keel and stern. Note that if building a double-ended boat, the bearding line will show on the sternpost as well.

With a Number 47 drill make two holes in the template (C) about a quarter of the way from each end. (These positions are not critical; they are merely register holes.) In the template (D) drill two similar holes a convenient distance from each end and, in this template only, drill holes with a Number 56 drill as near the edge as possible, one at the top of the bow, one at the forefoot, one at the foot of the stern, and if the template is for a double-ended boat, one at the top of the stern.

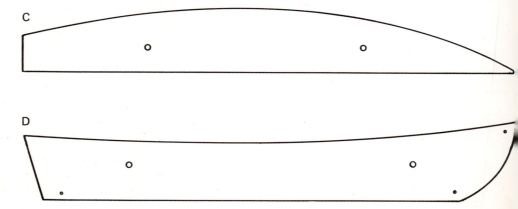

The half-breadth template (C) and the profile template (D).

Silver steel pegs about 1/2" long, which will fit exactly into the holes you have drilled, must now be made. The reason I have specified Numbers 47 and 56 drills is that Stubs silver steel can be purchased exactly to these dimensions; but if one has a stock of silver steel of nearly the same size with drills to correspond, there is no reason why this should not be used, for these sizes are not obligatory.

Now lay template (C) on the top of one of the half blocks and drill down into the block, using a Number 47 drill mounted in a vertical pillar drill, through the two holes, ensuring that the straight edge is flush with the inside edge of the block; turn the template over and similarly drill into the other half block. Do not drill too deeply otherwise the hole will penetrate

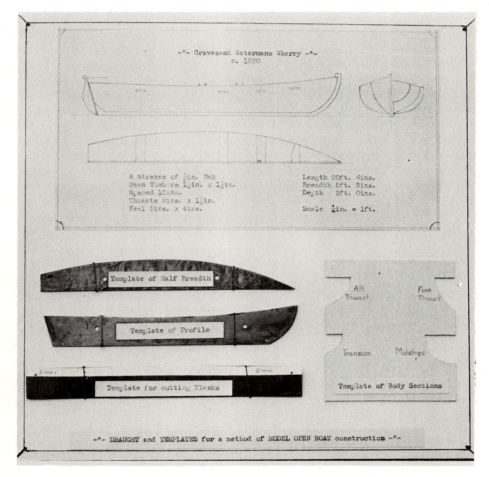

Another demonstration model by the Author explaining the building of the waterman's wherry. (Photograph by courtesy of John Bowen)

the hull when one comes to shape up the outside of the shell. Keeping the steel pegs in the holes to prevent movement, mark round with a hard sharp pencil the curved edge of the template on both blocks. Mark with a square a pencil line around each block at each end of the template; this will give the measurement of the extreme length of the shell. Take template (D) and placing it within the boundaries of the two lines that have just been drawn, on what will be the inside face of one of the half blocks, and with the bottom edge parallel to the bottom face, drill through the two larger holes into the block with the vertical pillar drill, again ensuring not to drill too deeply. Place pegs into the holes to hold the template steady and drill, with a Number 56 drill, through the remaining small holes vertically into the block. Do the same with the other block, making sure that the template has not been reversed, but that both bows are towards their correct ends.

Drill in the same manner, using template (D), through the piece of wood selected for the keel plate; in each case mark around the edge of the template with a hard sharp pencil. This will give the shape of the profile when one begins the carving of the hull.

One can now join together, by inserting the steel pegs, the two blocks and the keel plate, knowing full well that each part will correspond exactly with its fellow and that when the blocks have been shaped and the keel plate cut, the three parts must fit together perfectly because they have been drilled from and cut to the dimensions of the same template.

The next stage is to carve the outside of each half block to the contours of the shape of the hull. To do this, first cut each block of wood to the shape

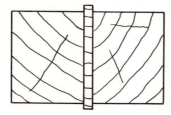

An end view of the hull blocks with the keel between.

of the profile template (D) taking care that the top curve (that is, the sheer) is at right angles to the inside face. The half-breadth template (C) can then be bent slightly to follow the sheer and have the pegs inserted to register its correct position; the outside curve must be re-marked and the block of wood cut to this mark.

One will then need to prepare templates, from the body plan drawing, of the vertical curve of the hull at various positions along its length. For a small boat four or five should be adequate and the templates can be made of thin, stiff card and positioned at the bow, midships and stern, the others at suitable places as the need arises. Each block can be shaped quite easily

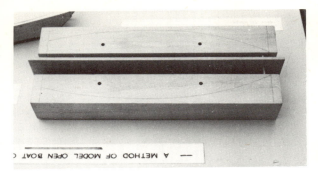

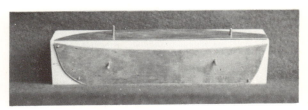
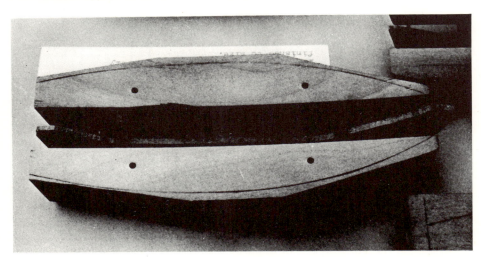

Various stages in the preparation of the hull blocks and keel piece, including the all-important use of templates. The middle two photographs depict a 26′ peter boat under construction but the others are of the waterman's wherry. (Photographs by courtesy of the Author and John Bowen)

by using chisels and gouges, and the shape checked by offering up a template at its particular position as the surplus is removed. Finally finish off with various grades of glasspaper to a smooth surface, taking care that the bow (and the stern in a double-ended boat) tapers off to a feather edge so that it flows sweetly into the stem. To aid in this, a dummy keel plate can be made which will save any possible damage to the one already made. As a point of interest, if one looks now at these curved outer surfaces the growth rings show as elongated elliptical rings, each block being the image of its mate.

It will be noticed that the small holes at the edges of the template now show as holes drilled through the edge of each half block; these holes will accommodate wood dowels when the time comes for glueing the shell together, the keel plate can be cut to shape at this stage, the inside edge to the finished line allowing for any deadwoods or sternposts, but the outside edge should be left full to save possible damage to it; this should be finished to the correct size as almost the last thing before painting. If the three parts are now re-assembled, making use of the silver steel pegs, an idea can be obtained of the appearance of the finished boat, and if necessary, corrections can be made to the shape of the hull if it is not perfectly symmetrical.

The next thing to do is to hollow out each half block to a thin shell, a job to which one must bring all available skill and care. Pencil a line about 1/8" or so inside the bearding line on the inside face of each half block; this is merely a line for guidance when finishing off. With suitable sized chisels and gouges remove from the inside as much as safety permits. When one has proceeded as far as possible with hand tools, the remainder is removed with the aid of rotary files. These are engineers' tools of various shapes and sizes used, amongst other purposes, for the cleaning up of metal castings. They are made in many cuts, from very coarse rasps to very fine abrasive rubber, but file cuts 1 or 2 are the most suitable.

For this purpose one can manage quite successfully with two of ball shape, say 3/4" and 1" diameter, but one of a pear shape about 1/2" diameter, and smaller sizes in the ball shape might prove useful, although these latter are not essential for one will obtain better results with either of the two larger balls for the major part of the work.

These rotary files are attached to a steel shaft of about 3/16" diameter which is held in the chuck of a vertical pillar drill or, less conveniently, in a horizontal position in the chuck of a lathe. Start with the larger ball (this can be used for the majority of the work) and have it spinning fairly fast; though this is a matter for experiment, about 3000 rpm is fine. Offer the half shell to the file. One will need to hold the work firmly in two hands so as to prevent damage by its slipping under the file, but one soon gets used to the feel of the job, Keep the work moving under the file so as not to burn the wood and also to avoid getting bumps and hollows which can be awkward to rectify. Use as large a ball as possible, otherwise a series of ridges and furrows which can be difficult to remove will result. Stop occasionally to test the thickness of the shell. Soon only a thin shell remains and by its feel, and by holding it up to the light, one can judge how much has been removed. Surprising as it may seem, with a boat such as the one I am describing, a thickness of 0.002" can quite easily be reached, and with practice

The hull after the hollowing out operation. (Photograph by courtesy of John Bowen)

even less. The shell of the 28'0" New Bedford Whaleboat, of which there is a photograph in the Introduction, has a thickness of 1/2", which, at a scale of 1/4" = 1'0", is 0.0011".

But to return to the job in hand: after using the large ball as much as possible it may be found convenient to change over to the smaller ball or to the pear shape to take out a bit more from the corners which the large ball cannot reach; after this use glasspaper of varying grades to finish off the surface as smoothly as possible.

There are now two half shells and a shaped central keel plate which have to be joined together; to do this, thin wood or split bamboo dowels must be substituted for the steel pins. These can be made by drawing the material through a series of diminishing holes drilled in a piece of tin-plate to reach the correct diameter. If the draw plate is held firmly in a vice, one can, in this way, make dowels of hair thickness for use when fixing other small parts on the hull.

Whenever I have given a practical demonstration of this method of model boat construction, I am asked without fail one question—What glue do you use?—as if there is some secret preparation known only to myself. I have always used one called 'Seccotine'. I find it holds extremely well, is clean in use and I have used it for years without any failure. However, if the reader has a familiar and favourite glue, it can be used instead, always assuming that it is a liquid fish glue type so as to allow for manipulation during assembly and not one of the quick setting, or 'pear drop' cements.

As all the holes have been drilled from the same template the three parts must fit together perfectly and so, after making sure that the edges to be glued are clean, run a little glue along the surfaces and on the keel plate, dip the dowels in glue and after pressing them into the dowel holes, one should find that the whole thing will hold together by only hand pressure; but spring clothes pegs or rubber bands at strategic points, though not necessary if the work has been done accurately, will help to hold the parts together while the glue dries. Use enough, but not too much glue; any surplus squeezed out can easily be removed with a damp cloth before it hardens.

When the glue is set (do not be in too much of a hurry, but leave as long as possible), clean up the boat inside and outside with fine glasspaper after cutting off the surplus of the dowels. Glue the hog into the bottom of the boat; this is a thin strip of wood 9" to 12" wide which covers the joints between the keel and the hull sides and so binds the hull sides together.

The thin shell is now completed. After the addition of the transom, this could be finished off to represent a carvel built boat, and later pages will contain details of how this is done.

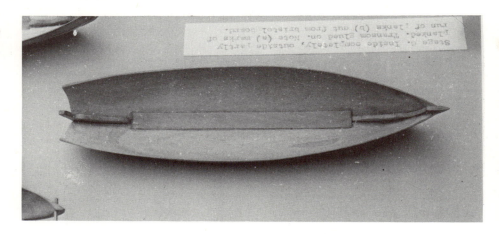

The two hollowed out halves of the hull fitted to the keel. (Photograph by courtesy of John Bowen)

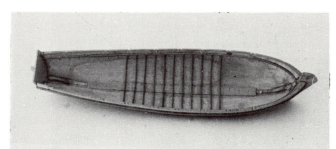

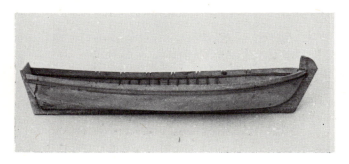

This technique can be used for all types of open boat—here is a model of the 'Victory's' gig under construction. (Photographs by courtesy of John Bowen)

CHAPTER 2

Planking the shell

As this is a clinker built boat the next stage is to start planking the shell. If one considers the skin of a boat it is obvious to see that the girth amidships is greater than that at the bow or stern, and therefore, to cover the surface with a number of identically shaped planks, each one will have to be wider in the middle than at each end. So the problem is to work out the shape of each plank. To do this, take a point at the position of greatest girth and others at the bow, the stern, and at two others conveniently spaced between them. Treating each half of the shell separately, measure the girth along a vertical line at each of these five points. Since this cannot be done with a rule or pair of dividers, take a narrow strip of paper and laying it along the line mark off with a very sharp pencil the measurement. Check each side against the other for there may be a slight discrepancy which one may be able to rectify (though if the work has been done accurately, each side should be identical).

There should now be five strips of paper of differing lengths, (these should be marked so that it is obvious to which position each strip refers) and they now have to be divided into a number of spaces corresponding to the number of planks. This may be anything from seven to thirteen or more and it is most unlikely that this could be done with an ordinary steel rule; it could be done with a pair of proportional dividers, but if one does not possess such an instrument there is quite an easy way out.

Take a piece of stiff, hard white card of which one corner must be a right angle; mark along the base equal spaces corresponding to the required number of planks, in this case eight, and join these points up to a common point at a convenient position along the perpendicular edge. Then it is obvious that if a line is drawn parallel to the base and across the eight slanting lines,

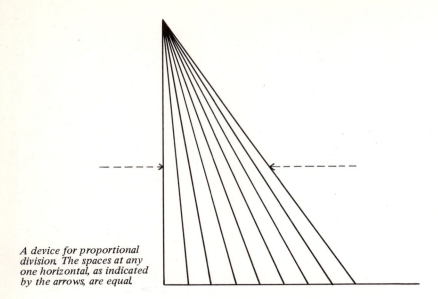

A device for proportional division. The spaces at any one horizontal, as indicated by the arrows, are equal.

it will itself be divided into eight equal parts. So take each of the five strips of paper, slide each one up the card parallel to the base and where its ends touch the ends of the chart, mark off eight equal spaces. This is best done, not with a pencil but, as a precise point is required, with a needle point set in a suitable holder.

Take each of the five strips and holding each one exactly in its respective place on the shell, prick through the marks into and through the shell. Thus one will obtain a mark inside and outside which is of minute size and cannot be obliterated. This gives the width of the plank as seen by an observer but, because each plank overlaps its neighbour, the actual width is slightly greater than is apparent.

The next thing to do is to cut the planks by means of a template, and though the planks vary in length all of them can be made using one template of brass which should be a little longer than the longest plank and about an inch in width, though this is not critical.

Scribe a line near one edge, but at least the distance from it of the widest

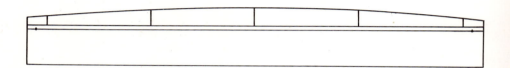

A template for cutting planks—the curve is exaggerated in this diagram.

part of the plank, that is, one of the spaces marked on the midships strip of paper. Erect five perpendiculars on this line at positions which correspond to the five marked on the shell. Mark on the template the bow and stern ends for future reference, and on the five perpendiculars the measurements which give the apparent width of the plank as I have explained, taken from each of the five strips at their appropriate places. Join these five points in a fair curve and file away the edge of the template to this curve. Now as each plank has to overlap its neighbour, scribe a line below the first line and about a quarter of the width of the plank away. At each end of the template, on this line, just beyond the extremities of the plank, drill a very small hole only large enough for a needle point to be pressed in and soldered in place so that its point protrudes slightly.

If the boat is to be painted, a suitable material to use for the planks is Bristol board. This is a hard white card obtainable from artists' suppliers and is sold as two sheet, three sheet or four sheet and so on, and it measures 0.009", 0.013" and 0.019" thick respectively. At a 1/4" = 1'0" this represents almost 1/2", 3/4" and 1". If the boat is to be finished as a varnished hull then another suitable material is a wood veneer backed with paper which is 0.005" thick. It is actually wood, and is used in the decorating trade as wallpaper and can be obtained in several different colours. The only disadvantage is that the grain is rather pronounced but by careful selection of parts of a sheet showing a closer grain, a better scale effect can be obtained. If it is necessary to increase the thickness it can be fixed to a backing of paper or Bristol board but a waterproof glue should be used to obviate the risk of separation in the subsequent operations.

Take the template and press it, needle points down onto the material being used for the planks, cut through the card, along the curved edge with a sharp knife at one stroke, lift off the template and one will see the two holes made by the needle points. Place a straight edge connecting these two marks and cut along the line. In this way one can continue to cut off identical planks ready to glue on to the shell, always remembering to mark the bow and stern ends, and the midships position.

As this is a model of a clinker built hull the inside as well as the outside must be planked, but since on the outside the upper planks overlap the lower ones, on the inside the reverse is the case and the lower planks appear to overlap the upper ones. Therefore, on the outside one must start at the bottom and work to the top, but on the inside, which is done first, it is necessary to start at the top and work towards the bottom.

Take one of the planks, cut off the bow end so that the amidships point registers correctly and then chamfer the bow end to a feather edge so that it will fit into the space between the shell and the stem, and having the straight edge of the plank uppermost. Dampen it with a small paint brush dipped in water so that it becomes pliable but not sodden, coat with a film

Opposite: Details of the planking of the waterman's boat—except the bottom photograph which, by way of contrast, shows the magnificent sweep of the planking on the bow of the Southwold beach yawl. (Photographs by courtesy of John Bowen)

of glue and fix it in place. There is no need to glue the first plank at the top of the shell, but lower down so that the upper edge lies along the line of the first row of needle points that have been marked through the shell. Temporarily, the end of the plank may be left sticking out at the stern as it is easier to cut it off later when everything is dry. Fix the corresponding plank in the same way to the opposite inside.

As the second row of holes has now been covered up, one must re-mark them by pricking through from the outside and through the plank that has just been fixed. Now glue in the second plank and proceed thus to each inside alternately until the bottom is reached.

While working, check that the planks are equally spaced as slight errors can creep in which, if not spotted at the time will show up only too clearly when it is too late to rectify matters.

If the work is done steadily and carefully, one may find that the upper plank will be dry enough by the time that the next lower plank is ready for fixing; but one should not be in too much of a hurry or else the previous plank will be disturbed. When the inside planking is completed and quite dry, one can then cut off the ends sticking out at the stern. Then one may glue on the transom using a piece of quarter sawn lime similar to that used for the keel plate. It is an advantage to fix this in place with split bamboo dowels for it will strengthen it greatly.

There is one point I should mention at this stage and that is, that if one is building a double-ended boat the planks must be cut to the exact length so as to fit between the stem and sternpost otherwise the procedure is similar. When everything is dry, the outside can be tackled, but first clean it up and see that the transom edges are flush with the sides.

It is as well, at this point, if it has not been done before, to examine a clinker built boat; for though many may think they know, it is probable that few know exactly how one is built. Hundreds of examples can be seen on rivers, lakes or drawn up on beaches anywhere the whole world over. Looking at the run of the planking, one will see that each plank is rabbetted into the stem and also into each other as they approach it, so that the overlap gradually diminishes from about 6" to 9" from the hooded ends, and so at

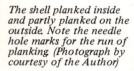

The shell planked inside and partly planked on the outside. Note the needle hole marks for the run of planking. (Photograph by courtesy of the Author)

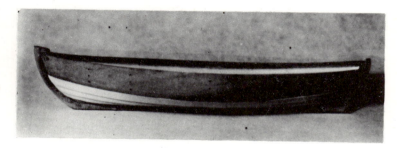

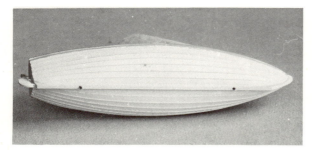

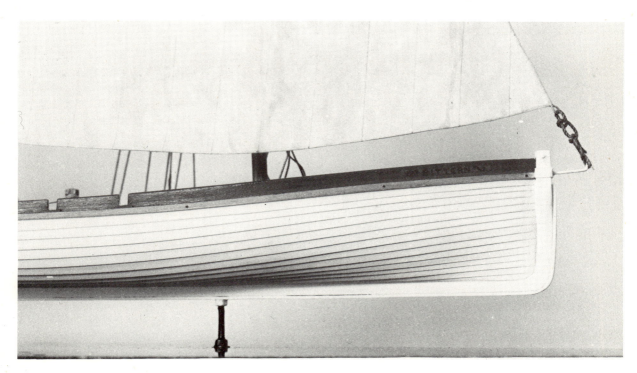

the stem itself, the surface of the planks becomes smooth as in a carvel hull. The same applies at the stern, if it is a double-ended boat; but a transom-ended boat preserves the overlap. This is one of those details which, though small, makes all the difference in the construction of a first class model.

In planking the outside one should start at the bottom and the first plank to fix is glued above the first row of needle holes. Cut the plank to correct length so that the amidships point registers exactly in place and shave off the bow end to a feather edge. Glue it on so that the straight edge of the plank runs along the line of the needle holes and the bow end runs smoothly into the stem with no trace of a bump. Do the same on the other side. As the second row of needle holes is now covered up, they must be re-marked before one can fix the second plank. At the bow end the overlap should fade away into the rabbet of the stem as I have pointed out, and the planks should be in a gentle curve. This will require some care but the glue will make it possible to adjust the run of the planking before it grips. Proceed thus on alternate sides up to the gunwale where, if the measuring has been done accurately the last plank should fit the last space exactly.

Trim off the ends sticking out beyond the transom and when dry the planks may be smoothed off with very fine glasspaper. Note that, if there is a rubber just below the gunwale, it may be unnecessary to glue on the last plank up to the top of the shell. Now glue the gunwale itself in place along the top edges and finish off with fine glasspaper to correspond with the line of the sheer.

Having finished the planking clean up the inside and the outside to remove dirty finger marks, and surplus glue if any, by gently washing over with a paint brush dipped in water. Do not use too much otherwise the planks may lift. If this does happen, glue must be worked in beneath them to re-fix them.

CHAPTER 3

Fitting out and displaying the model

When everything is dry, it is as well to apply a coat of paint to both the inside and the outside. Thin the paint down to a consistency of almost that of milk and it will run into all the crevices without adding materially to the thickness or leaving unsightly brush marks. When the paint is dry, and not before, one can start fixing the timbers. For these there is no better wood than apple, if it can be acquired (though hornbeam or lime will make good substitutes). It can be reduced to amazingly small scantlings, even as small as 0.005" square, without collapse and can be bent to small curves without risk of fracture; furthermore, if the wood is sawn on the full quarter, when it is bent it will not twist. For the boat under construction the timbers are 1 1/8" moulded by 1 1/2" sided, which at this scale is 0.023" by 0.030", and when the wood has been converted to these dimensions one will find that it can be bent easily to the curves of the hull though if any difficulty is experienced, soaking in water will make the task easier. If one slips the ends under the gunwales, after cutting the strips of wood exactly to size, the tension will hold them in close contact with the planks with no adhesive necessary; subsequent painting will make them immovable.

The first timber to go in is that amidships and when it has been satisfactorily fixed one can then work fore and aft, spacing the other timbers at the prescribed distance apart of 1'3", but where the deadwoods are, at the bow and stern, each timber will be in two halves.

When all the timbers are fixed, glue in the breast hook and stern hooks if there are any shown on the drawings. Next, glue over the timbers, at the correct height from the gunwales, the thwart clamps, which should extend to just beyond the thwarts, holding them in place until the glue is dry with the aid of spring clothes pegs; also to be fixed, if there are any, are stringers

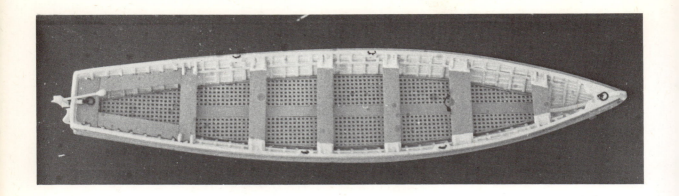

The interior fittings of an open boat. Note the timbers, stringers, thwarts, stern-sheets and the bottom board gratings that are the mark of a naval boat in the age of sail. (Photographs by courtesy of John Bowen)

which are placed in the bilges. Neither the thwart clamps nor the stringers, if any, should depend upon the glue alone, but should be fixed, additionally with two or more very fine dowels.

When all is securely attached and dry is the time to paint the inside to a finished state. The best paint to use is a high quality one of a matt or egg-shell texture, and normally this should be white, though sometimes pastel shades are used, as in the whaleboat, which was pale green or pale blue. Thin it down with suitable thinners almost to the consistency of thick milk; in this way the paint will fill all the crevices and several coats can be applied, taking care that each coat is dry before applying the next, without materially increasing the thickness and at the same time eliminating all brush marks and blobs of paint.

When the finish is satisfactory, one should then fix the bottom boards; these may be fore and aft, open or close boarding or sometimes placed athwartships (according to the prototype). A good way is to cut a thin card or paper pattern of the bottom of the boat on which one can assemble the boards and so prefabricate the unit for fixing in place on suitably spaced cross members. Glasspaper the boards to a fine finish as these, and also the thwarts (which are the next item to be considered), are never painted but left bare to guard against the risk of the feet of the rowers slipping, as they might do on a painted surface. The thwarts themselves should be cut to the correct size 8″ by 1 3/8″, that is 0.166″ by 0.025″ at this scale and of such length that they fit exactly without being loose or having to be forced into place, so pressing out the sides of the hull.

At each end of the thwarts are fixed the thwart knees. There may be one or sometimes two at each end and are usually made of wood, though occasionally they may be of metal. If thin wood is used for them, one may find that as they are so small they will split; therefore the best material to use is white celluloid or plastic (collar stiffeners make ideal material). Cut them with a sharp knife and file them to shape. Glue them in place and when all are secured, paint them and the ends only of the thwarts up to the ends of the knees.

If there are any thwart pillars these can now be added and also the rowing stretchers. The thwart pillars were placed in the middle of the thwarts to support them and were usually in the form of a turned baluster; but do not make them too clumsy. The rowing stretchers were either a bar or a board against which the rower placed his feet. This should complete the interior of the boat unless there are any other minor fittings such as eyebolts or davit rings in the prototype which are needed.

With regard to the exterior, firstly trim off the excess from the bottom of the keel, shape the stem to the correct curve and feather off the leading edge, though not to a knife edge. When all is done to satisfaction and cleaned up, paint the exterior as for the interior and when dry, scrape off any paint from the rubber to leave the wood bare; then fit the rowlocks or thole pins, whichever is correct for the particular type of boat. Thole pins

The Southwold beach yawl 'Bittern,' its internal fittings and rigging. (Photographs by courtesy of John Bowen)

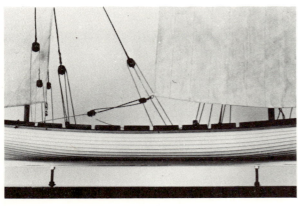

Right: *The completed boat with a figure to give an idea of scale.*
Opposite: *Two ideas for the displaying of the finished model—the top one is a 'below bridges' type of peter boat shown lying on a stylised stretch of foreshore; in contrast, the Thames wherry is part of a scene complete with figures. (Photographs by courtesy of the Author)*

can be made of pins or wire not more than 0.020" diameter which is 1" to scale, but rowlocks will need to be made by hard soldering a semi-circular shaped piece of wire to a straight piece, and inserted into a tiny hole drilled into the gunwale about 1'3" ahead of the appropriate thwart.

The rudder can now be made out of a piece of thin wood and hung from the sternpost using pins for pintles (incidentally entomological pins can be purchased; made of hard brass wire of all thicknesses from 0.005" diameter upwards, they are invaluable for scale size work). Gudgeons are made from nickel silver sheet or copper foil. There is usually one pintle and one gudgeon on each of the rudder and sternpost and the drawing will give their positions. Paint the assembly to match the boat and when hung, fit the tiller or the crosshead with ropes, whichever is correct.

Little else should remain to be done except to consider the display of the model. If it has been made to be placed on the skids on the deck of a ship there is no problem; otherwise several ways can be considered. It can be supported on a baseboard, in the traditional way, on small brass pillars or on crutches or perhaps one might like to be a bit more imaginative and hang it from a pair of davits. Another way would be to make a baseboard to

1820 ESTUARY TYPE PETER BOAT ¼IN = 1FT

A good model requires no displaying, as with this waterman's boat, but the action diorama must offer the best opportunities to a modeller with imagination—the spectacular whalehunt, below, is a fine example, (Photograph by courtesy of the Author)

represent part of the deck of a ship and lash it down on skids. Consideration might be given to a scenic model by making a pebble beach or sandy shore and laying the boat on its bilges surrounded by suitable equipment such as nets and so forth if it is a fishing boat, or ropes and perhaps an anchor if more applicable. However, one should give the artistic sense full play and make the most of a delightful model.

Representative open boats

CHAPTER 4

Aldeburgh boats

An 18' boat on Aldeburgh beach. Note the hook from the stemhead and the sacks of ballast. (Photograph by courtesy of the Author)

Aldeburgh is a small town on the Suffolk coast between Lowestoft and Clacton. All that remains of the old town now is the High Street separated from the foreshore by a narrow street of houses. It was at one time a flourishing port with a history stretching back to the Domesday Book, and contributed its quota with that of Dunwich (now almost entirely engulfed by the sea) to the naval force raised against the Spanish Armada, as well as figuring again and again in the maritime history of England.

Within living memory it boasted its own fleet of wet well cod fishing smacks, but the town over the centuries has been fighting a losing battle against the erosion of the coast by the sea, and the silting up with tons and tons of shingle of the entrance to the harbour at Slaughden at the southern end of the town. Consequently the larger fishing vessels have gone northwards to Lowestoft and Great Yarmouth, and the only fishing done now is by small open boats, a dozen or more of which can be seen drawn up on the steeply shelving, stoney beach.

These boats make an interesting study for those who have a liking for East Anglian beach boats. But, as is happening elsewhere nowadays, they are undergoing a change, though whether they will ever disappear entirely is a debatable point. They vary in size from about 15'0" to 20'0" in length, and are used for trawling, drifting or line fishing, and also for catching lobsters and crabs according to the season. When at work they rarely go out of sight of land.

On the beach at varying times (depending upon the state of the tide) there is always an old fisherman getting the boats ready for the two man crews. He will put aboard all the gear required for the particular purpose, whether trawling or netting, and then he will do a curious thing. He will start to fill several small sacks with shingle off the beach, often aided by any little boy visitor on holiday, and then pack them into the bottom of the boat. The purpose of this is twofold; firstly it acts as ballast on the trip out and secondly, as the fish are caught it is the means of lightening the boat, for the shingle is simply tipped overboard and the catch becomes the ballast,

Hauling the 18' boat up the beach. The nets can just be seen on the extreme left. (Photographs by courtesy of the Author)

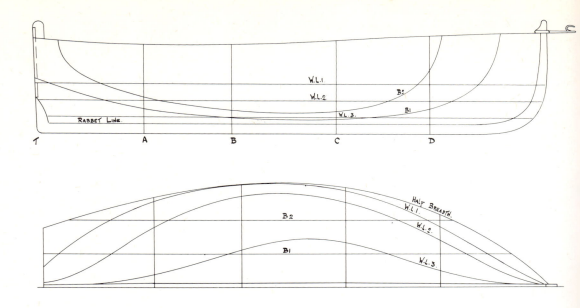

The lines plan of the Aldeburgh boat 'Ossie'. (By courtesy of the Science Museum, London. Unless otherwise stated, all of the representative open boat plans are from that source.)

the empty sacks being brought back, of course, for refilling on the next occasion.

Practically all the boats are driven by small petrol engines. Some of those of more recent construction have been built as motor-sailers, but many are obvious conversions of older sailing-rowing boats, having the propeller shaft located to one side of the sternpost. Just a few have remained as they were originally, but all of them, generally speaking, are of similar build, differing only in minor detail.

The most striking features about them are the low ratio of length to beam, which is about two and a half to one, and the heaviness of the construction, which is of clinker laid larch planks on sawn frames with keel and posts of oak. Undoubtedly this had been found to be necessary because of the buffeting which they receive from the sea, and the wear and tear caused by operating from an open beach. They are pushed down into the sea, and on their return are dragged back up again by means of rather primitive capstans or manually operated winches. Large section gunwales are fitted inside the top strake with a rubbing strake on the outside for added strength and with two or three bilge keels to protect the planking when the boat lies on the beach. There are usually three or four thwarts, each with two knees and lodging knees, and thole pins are fitted for rowing in an emergency; the whole effect is one of tremendous strength for so small a boat.

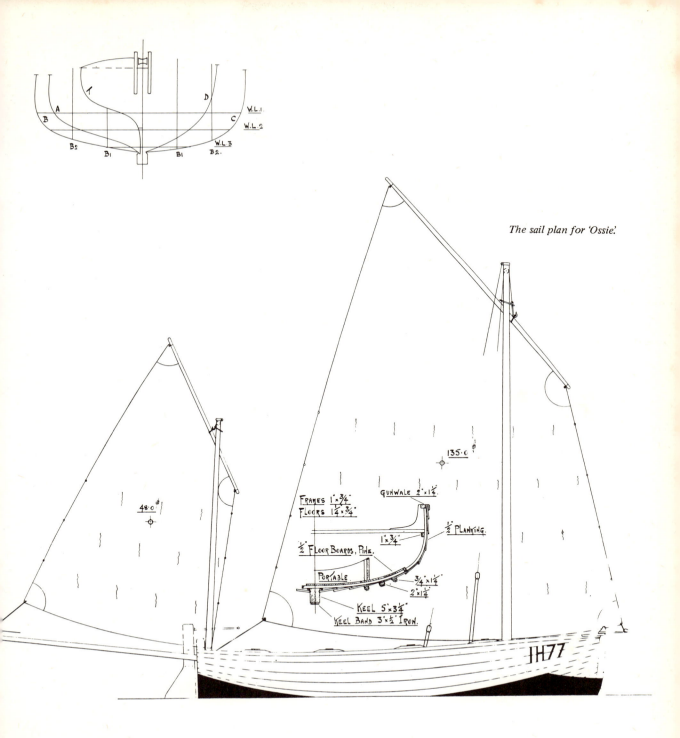

The sail plan for 'Ossie'.

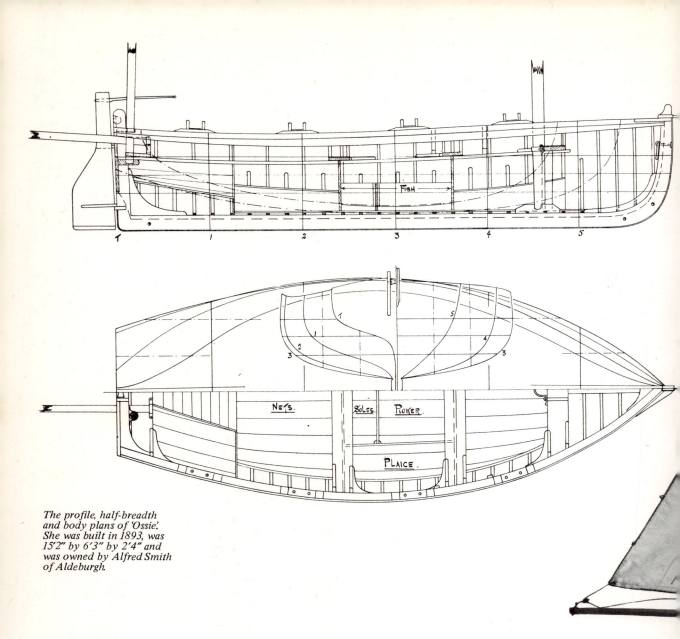

The profile, half-breadth and body plans of 'Ossie'. She was built in 1893, was 15'2" by 6'3" by 2'4" and was owned by Alfred Smith of Aldeburgh.

The Science Museum model of 'Ossie'. (Photograph by courtesy of Martin Treadway)

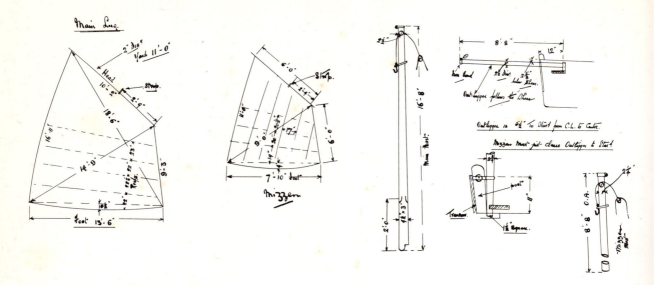

Sketches of the spars and sails. These are not to scale.

The men are evidently as tough as the boats they sail, for I have seen them go out in all weathers, and on one occasion put out in a fog or sea mist which swallowed them up when scarcely more than a few feet from the water's edge.

The space inside the boat is entirely undecked but has provision for a fore mast carrying a lugsail, and a mizen mast stepped at the transom for a riding lugsail. Bottom boards are fixed over the floors and there is also an arrangement of boards set up on edge to serve as fish pounds; into these the various sorts of fish, such as plaice, sole and ray, are separated. Where the boat has been fitted with a motor these pounds are not so much in evidence, presumably there is not sufficient time for the fish to be sorted, for while the boats are chugging back to shore the men are kept busy tidying up the gear and washing the nets.

As the boat nears the shore the engine is kept running until the last moment and the boat hits the beach with an alarming crash, whereupon a wire rope from the winch is quickly shackled to a ring at the foot of the stem, and the boat is hauled up just above the tidemark.

The fish are unloaded onto the beach and sorted and gutted, to the accompaniment of the screams of the gulls which have followed the boat to the shore. Then, once the requirements of the local hotels and shops had been met, one used to be able to buy fish as fresh as is humanly possible. After this, the boat is washed out and generally tidied up and then hauled up the beach to above the high water mark, when wedges are slipped under the bilges to keep it on an even keel.

Only once in recent years have I seen one of these boats under sail, yet all have an iron bumkin about 12″ long ending in a hook protruding from the stem head for the attachment of the fore stay. This would appear nowadays to be rather unneccessary and almost of a vestigial character since sails are hardly ever used, and are rarely stowed aboard with the other gear.

Little variation in colouring is seen, for the boats are usually painted white inside and outside with a blue top strake and a black bottom. Registration letters and numbers are painted on the bows, and sometimes the name of the boat and of the owner is carved on the transom on each side of the rudder.

One photograph shows a model I made of one of the old sailing-rowing type, with the fish pounds and all inside gear fitted. The others show the present day type; these are some 18′0″ long, fitted with a motor, and illustrate what little change has taken place besides showing the lines of the boats. In the foreground is a 15′0″ trawl beam with the net laid out to dry, while in the far background can be seen a boat tipped on its bilges to show the interior layout.

A very fine and fully detailed set of draughts of a boat 15′0″ long, built in 1893, can be obtained from the National Maritime Museum, Greenwich, London, SE10; a photograph of this draught can be obtained from the Science Museum, London, SW7.

Typical equipment for Aldeburgh boats: lobster pots (left) and nets. (Photographs by courtesy of the Author)

CHAPTER 5

Lowestoft shrimping boats

Previous pages: Pre-War Lowestoft – unloading sprats in Lowestoft harbour from a beach boat similar to the 'Pride of the West'; a fine shot of the underwater body of one of these Lowestoft craft, with others in the background. Modellers who can achieve exhibition standard paint jobs should take notice of the standard of the real thing! (Photographs by courtesy of the Port of Lowestoft Research Society.
Above: A beach scene with a number of these craft drawn up.

Lowestoft on the Suffolk coast is now a large and busy fishing centre and though many of the smaller fishing boats have vanished, a few of the local shrimping boats, the remnants of a thriving industry and now fitted with a motor, may be seen hauled up on the beach or lying alongside the quay. The accompanying draught from the National Maritime Museum is of a transom stern Shrimp boat of some fifty years ago, 20'6" long with a beam of 8'0", and shows the boat as converted to a motor auxiliary.

Originally the majority of these boats set a loose-fitted, gaff mainsail with a foresail set on a bowsprit, but after conversion they appeared with a dipping lug sail forward and a mizen aft of almost a triangular shape with a small head yard, though its boom is reminiscent of the Yarmouth boats, the sail being sheeted to an outrigger.

The draught could be the basis for building a colourful model, since the sails were tanned with a mixture of red ochre and oil similar to, but not so heavily as, the sails of a Thames barge. The top strake of the hull was black, the bottom red and the remainder of the hull grey.

The boats were very strongly built for their size, being clinker built of thirteen oak strakes, 3/4" thick on closely spaced frames on a keel deepened by the addition of a false keel, and totalling 12" by 4" wide. They had also a thick gunwale 4" by 2" and a lower rubbing strake of 2 1/2" by 2".

A tiny cabin in the fore peak, occupying a third of the length, was decked over, the remainder being open but with bottom boards over the permanently stowed iron ballast. This particular boat had a crew of only one man but worked a 15'0" trawl.

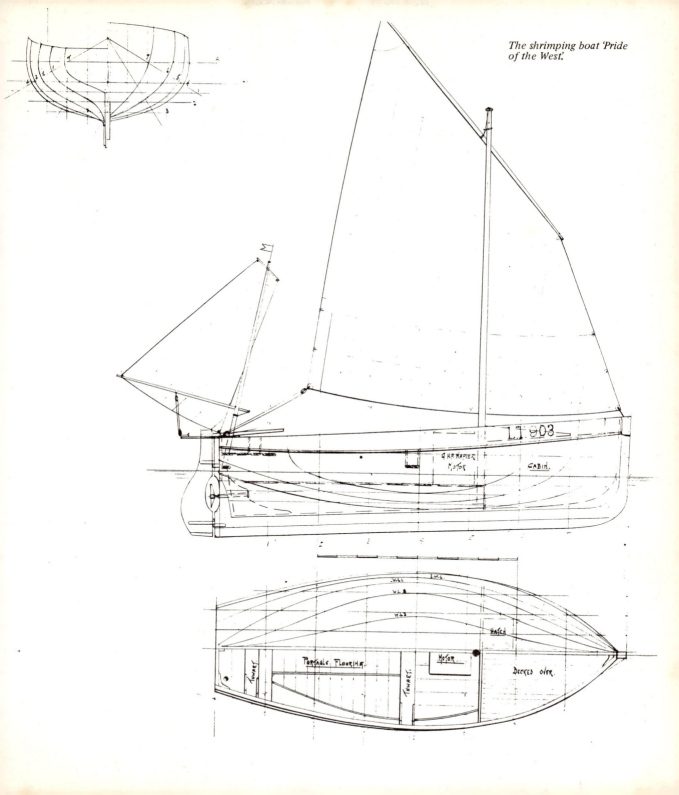

The shrimping boat 'Pride of the West'.

CHAPTER 6

Cobles

Right: *The Yorkshire coble 'Gratitude' at Whitby.*
Opposite: *The old harbour of Whitby crammed with cobles and other small sailing craft. (Photographs by courtesy of Conway Picture Library)*

It is easy to generalize and say that all cobles are the same, for basically this is so since the Northumbrian and Yorkshire types are similar; but they also have differences which provoke enthusiasts to fierce arguments as to which is the true original. They do not conform to one pattern but differ as local conditions have dictated. For example, there is a double-ended type which is a later development and is, in some ways, an improvement. In this, a sharp raking stern is substituted for the traditional flat transom, and it also has a normal projecting keel curved upwards at the after end in the same way as the typical coble. But in spite of these minor

Opposite: Fishing cobles at Seaham, Durham. (Photograph by courtesy of the Author)
Left: The Filey sailing coble 'Joan & Robin taken in 1955. (Photograph by courtesy of H Oliver Hill)

differences the coble—pronounced 'cobble' if you are a Yorkshireman—is a striking illustration of the influence of coastal conditions on the design of small inshore fishing craft. The East Coast cobles are unique, except for a class of fishing sampans, on the other side of the world, in Japan, where conditions are to be found similar to those which exist from the Humber to Berwick; in both areas there are few harbours, and the open boat has to be launched bow first from the beach into a rough sea or in the face of heavy breakers. So a craft has been evolved with sharp bows, a deep forefoot, a flat after body, and a long projecting rudder which acts as a subsidiary keel.

Though they may be magnificent sea boats (for it was in one of these that Grace Darling performed her memorable rescue from the *Forfarshire* in 1838), they require a great skill in their handling, an art acquired by the fishermen only after long experience. Unfortunately times are changing and it is an undoubted fact that the coble is fast disappearing; those few that are being built have a small petrol or diesel engine installed in a special way to which I shall refer later.

From the draught it will be seen that the coble has a pronounced sheer forward giving a very high bow with a deep forefoot, but that the stern is low and ends in a flat transom raked at a shallow angle. In consequence the curve of the gunwale gives the boat a most graceful appearance. Another striking feature of the coble is the relatively few strakes, some having only five broad full length planks and two short planks of about half the length. These, being laid clinker fashion, produced a pronounced tumble-home, and a hollow bow with the minimum beam at the lower edge of the top strake. There was no keel such as one normally associates with the word but a central member known as the ram plank, which is joined to the stem.

When building a coble the stem, which projects very little from the hooded ends of the planks, is rabetted for the planks; these are usually cut from larch or oak, and then the ram plank, fashioned from a substantial baulk of timber, is joined to it. It is similar in shape to a knife on edge at the forward end but gets broader and flatter further aft until it resembles a thick plank laid flat as the transom is reached. The planks are then laid from the bottom upwards, these deciding the ultimate form of the hull, for the frames, or timbers, are not added until the planking is completed. Then the timbers, sawn out of oak are fitted to the planks which, because of their widths, produce an angular contour to an athwartship section. The thwarts, mast and rudder complete the fitting out.

After a fishing trip the vessel, as it nears the shore, is turned so that the stern is facing the beach. The rudder, which as the draught shows extends well below the ram plank, acts almost as a centreboard, and is fitted with a very long curved tiller coming within easy reach of the helmsman. It is unshipped. Then waiting for a suitable opportunity, the coble is borne shorewards on the crest of a wave and beached stern first.

An Elizabethan author — and this shows that the coble has an exceedingly long history, — graphically describes this manoeuvre in the following way:
" . . . . but they, acquainted with these seas espying a broken wave reddy to overtake them, suddenly oppose the prowse of the boate to ytt and mounting on top decent as it were into a vally, hovering until they espy a whole wave coming rowling, which they observe commonly to be an odd one; where upon mounting with their coble as it were a great and furious horse they row with might and mayne and together with the wave drive themselves ashore."

Though it is said at times that cobles have twin keels this is not strictly accurate, for the two iron-shod skids, called the 'draughts' or 'skorvels', fitted to the bottom after part of the hull and which curve part way up the transom, are there for the purpose of protecting the boat when it is being beached, and when it is being hauled up above high water mark. Additionally they prevent the boat from overturning when resting on the beach. Cobles are always beached stern first and hauled up by means of wire ropes running from a winch to eye plates on the after sides of the top strakes; also, they are always towed stern first, for then the deep fore-foot acts as a rudder and prevents the boat yawing.

At present practically all remaining cobles are fitted with motors so that, in spite of their characteristic form having been developed for the purpose of hauling them up the beach, there is now a tendency for the vessels to be tied up to moorings in harbours or alongside quays whenever possible. If a motorized coble has to be beached the propeller shaft is fitted with lifting gear. This consists of a rod which passes through a watertight gland fitted in the bottom of the boat at the after end. The shaft has a universal joint so that when the rod is raised the propeller and shaft lie between the draughts or skorvels, and thus are protected whilst the vessel is being hauled up the beach.

The normal rig is one tall mast, raked aft, standing in a socket and held by a clamp to a thwart. The sail was a large dipping lug, tanned to a colour similar to that of a Thames barge, laced to a yard and hoisted by a halliard running through a sheave in the mast head; the tack and sheet at the lower corners were passed through holes in the top strake. Bowlines were sometimes provided, and with these the craft could sail unusually close to the wind. Oars, which were not always carried, were about 14′0″ in length. A narrow blade was clenched to a heavy, square sectioned loom which widened out and through it a hole was pierced, or a ring was fitted on to it, or a rope grommet made on it to allow it to pivot on a single thole pin on the gunwale.

Cobles were sometimes varnished outside but more often were painted in traditional bands of light colour, though, as a visit to Whitby will show, they are now painted in many different ways: so are the interiors, though red bottom boards and light blue sides seem to be the most popular.

These craft were used mainly for long line fishing and with a crew of three men could handle nearly two miles of line. They could have a carrying capacity of as much as one ton, and this in a boat which varied little as regards the length of 28′0″ and a beam of 6′0″ to 7′0″.

Launching a Filey coble. (Photograph by courtesy of H Oliver Hill)

Two views of the Science Museum model of a coble, showing the unusual shape of the hull in both plan and profile. (Photographs by courtesy of Martin Treadway)

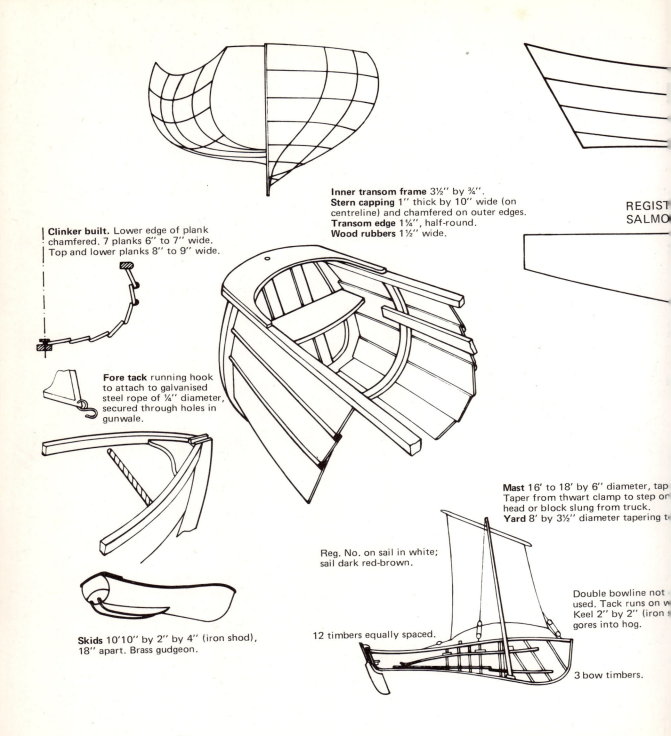

Inner transom frame 3½" by ¾".
Stern capping 1" thick by 10" wide (on centreline) and chamfered on outer edges.
Transom edge 1¼", half-round.
Wood rubbers 1½" wide.

Clinker built. Lower edge of plank chamfered. 7 planks 6" to 7" wide. Top and lower planks 8" to 9" wide.

Fore tack running hook to attach to galvanised steel rope of ¼" diameter, secured through holes in gunwale.

Mast 16' to 18' by 6" diameter, tap Taper from thwart clamp to step or head or block slung from truck.
Yard 8' by 3½" diameter tapering t

Reg. No. on sail in white; sail dark red-brown.

Double bowline not used. Tack runs on w Keel 2" by 2" (iron s gores into hog.

12 timbers equally spaced.

3 bow timbers.

Skids 10'10" by 2" by 4" (iron shod), 18" apart. Brass gudgeon.

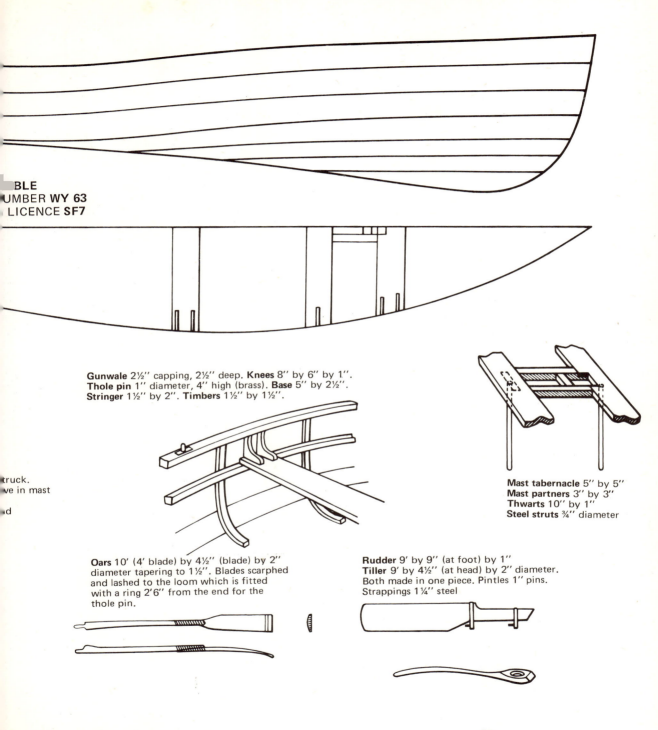

Previous pages: Constructional drawings prepared by the Author for his coble model. Redrawn by E N Wilson.
Right: An unusual bow shot of a Northumbrian coble owned by the Amble Pilots. (Photograph by courtesy of Conway Picture Library).
The plans on this and the following pages are of the Yorkshire coble 'Eliza': on this page is the sail plan, and opposite are the midship section, the profile, deck, and body plans.

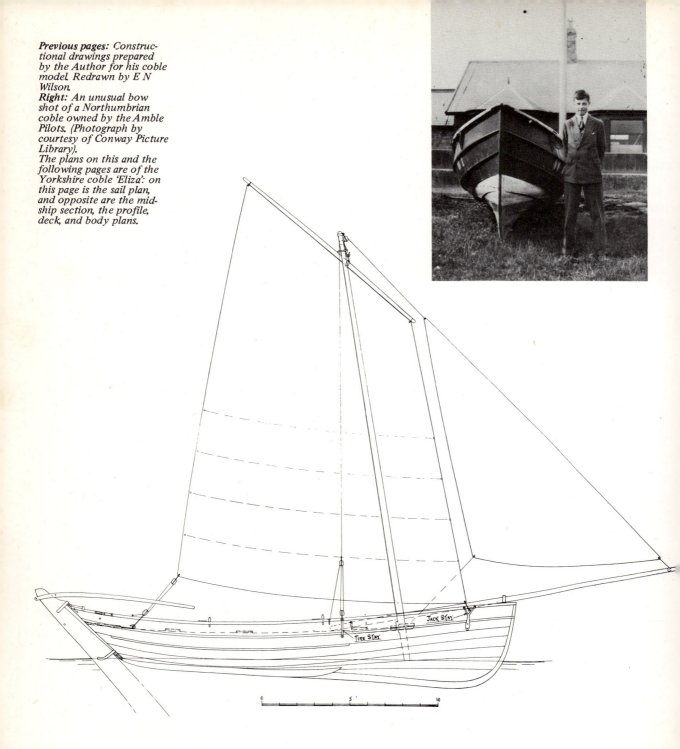

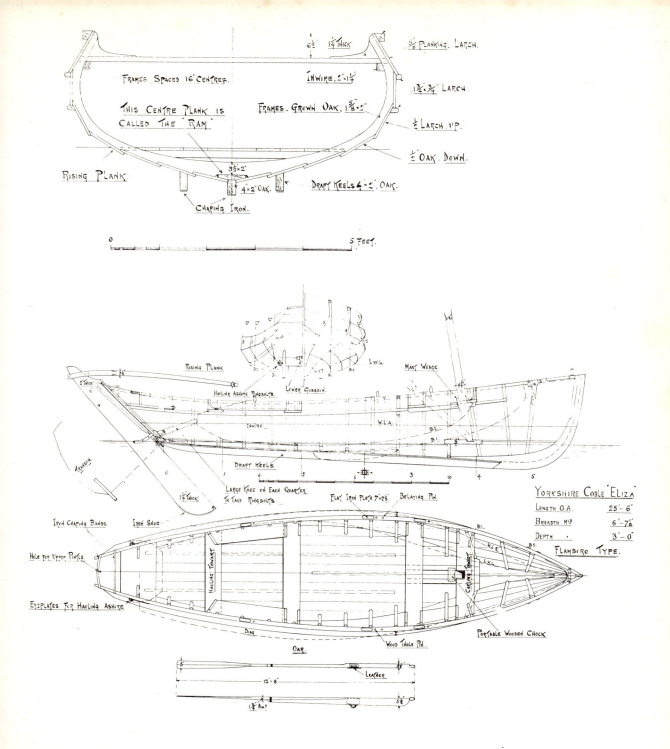

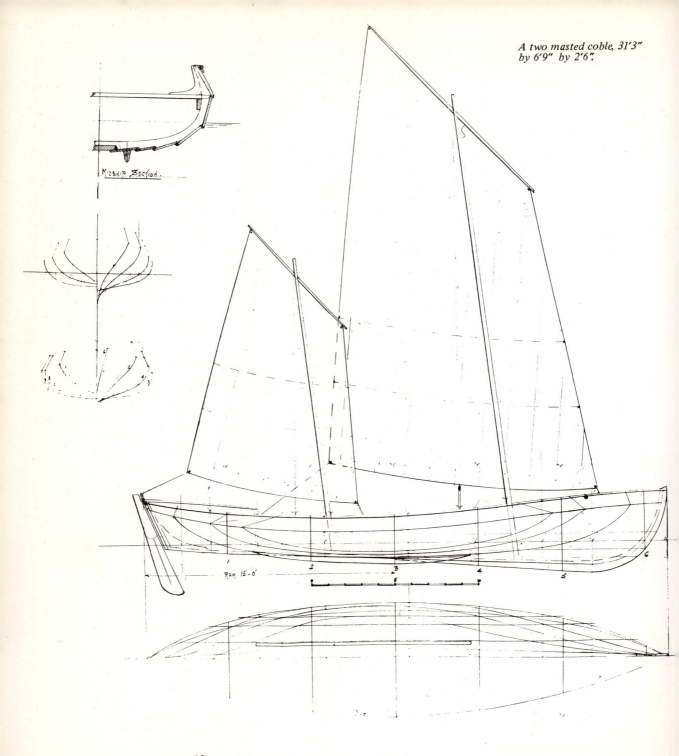

A two masted coble, 31'3" by 6'9" by 2'6".

CHAPTER 7

Sheringham crabbing boats

Sheringham is a little fishing village on the north Norfolk coast. In former times the crab boats were in common use there between Wells-next-the-sea and Cromer, and as with so many local boats they have developed peculiarities of construction which are the result not only of tradition but also of the coastal conditions and the purpose for which they were used. In some ways they are similar to the small above bridges type of peter boats and the Medway dobles (except for the partial decking of these) but little can be stated with any authority concerning the ancestry of inshore fishing craft, for such familiar objects offered little or no attraction to maritime historians. However all the available evidence supports the conclusion that these double-ended open boats owe their origin to the Norwegian yole.
In the Sheringham boat, lightness was the great essential and to achieve this some features of normal boatbuilding were omitted which, one would think, would have weakened the boat considerably; however this does not necessarily follow.
The accompanying photograph is of a draught in the National Maritime Museum and is of a crab boat built at Sheringham in 1912. It was 18'8" long with a wide beam of 5'6". The draught is fully detailed and from it it is possible to build an authentic model, though one or two peculiarities are worth noting. For instance, there are no gunwales, no keelson, no bottom boards and the alternate timbers (commonly, but erroneously, called the ribs) are left out at the bow and stern, although there are three short bilge keels for protection when on the beach. Built originally of oak, later boats such as this one were planked with larch 1/2" thick, as this facilitated the repair of damage caused by working amongst rocks. In spite of this they were surprisingly strong for this particular boat has carried 3600 mackerel and

61

The Science Museum model of the Sheringham crabber in its realistic setting—in point of fact the boat was rarely carried in this fashion, but the model would not stand when the more common method was tried. (Photograph by courtesy of Martin Treadway)

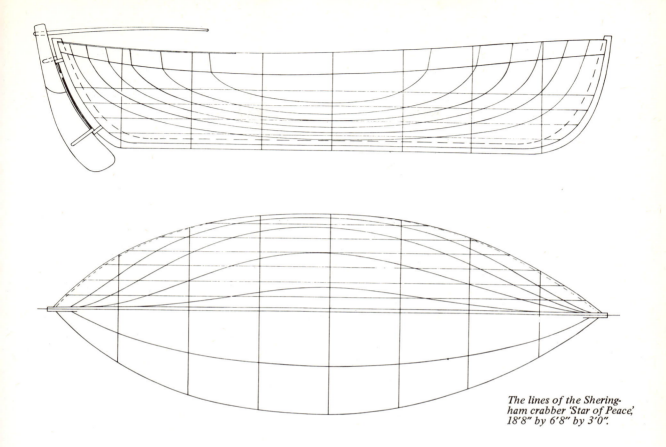

The lines of the Sheringham crabber 'Star of Peace', 18'8" by 6'8" by 3'0".

on another occasion 13 cwts of whelks. Amidships was a removeable parting board to prevent the ballast (collected in sacks from the beach in the same way as for the Aldeburgh sprat boats and necessary in view of the shallow draught) from shifting. A stern grating was used only when long line fishing, and was removed when crabbing or whelking. The rudder, which fitted the curved sternpost, projected below the keel as can be seen and is in the tradition of the Yorkshire cobles; it was of course easily hung or unshipped when near the shore.

Another interesting and peculiar feature of the boats is the oar ports. These were cut in the sheer strake and the oars were passed through them from outboard when working. The reason for this is apparent when the method of landing is described. The boat is beached broadside on. She is sailed straight for the beach and at the moment she is about to strike, the helm is put hard down bringing her round parallel with the shore, which she touches broadside on; the sail is lowered at the same time, a bag of ballast is thrown across the inside bilge so that the boat heels towards the land and the crew jumps out. The sea breaks under the seaward side of the boat and she is left to knock up the beach out of harm's way. Then the oars are passed right through the corresponding ports in each side of the boat, thus enabling it to be carried up the beach by four or six men.

The rig was a single mast set well forward and carrying a large dipping lug sail, the foot of which was almost as long as the boat itself. It was hoisted on a long yard and the tack led to a hook on the stemhead, the sheet being passed through a hole in the head of the sternpost. Normally, the boats were either painted white all over or varnished on the natural wood.

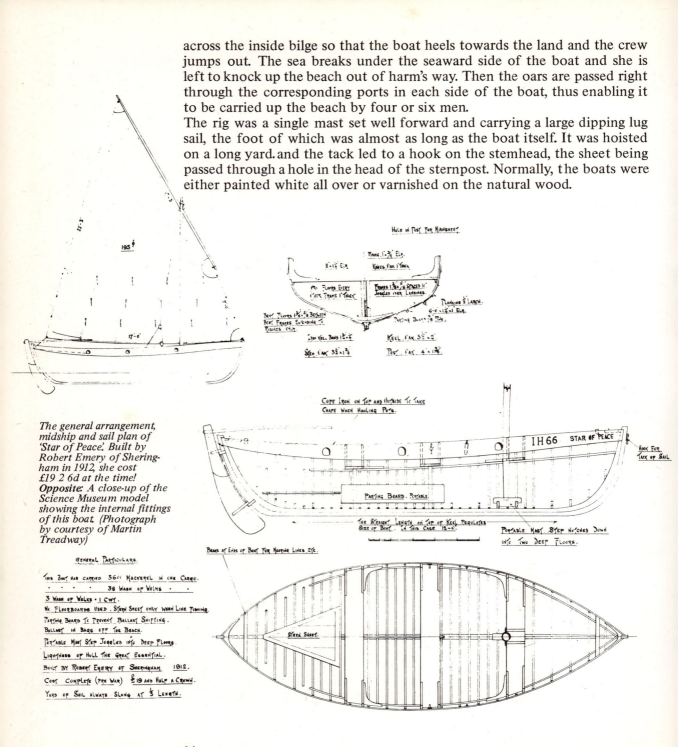

The general arrangement, midship and sail plan of 'Star of Peace'. Built by Robert Emery of Sheringham in 1912, she cost £19 2 6d at the time!
Opposite: *A close-up of the Science Museum model showing the internal fittings of this boat. (Photograph by courtesy of Martin Treadway)*

CHAPTER 8

Peter boats

Thames peter boats are—or rather were—small open fishing boats, for they are no longer to be seen; yet it is only within living memory that they have disappeared, for as late as 1901 two could be seen at Putney—and this after a history extending for a thousand years. The legend tells that when King Edward the Confessor's first Abbey Church of Westminster was to be consecrated about the year 1000 AD, a fisherman was tending his boat on the opposite bank of the river. He was accosted by a venerable looking old man who asked to be ferried across to the other side. As the strange traveller landed the windows of the church were filled with light and heavenly music issued from the building, and thus by Peter, for it was none other than the Saint himself, was the church consecrated. No fee did the saintly traveller leave for the poor fisherman but a blessing for such as he.

Now whether or not one believes the story is of little consequence, as it is obvious that the name must derive in some way from that of the patron saint of all fishermen, and I suppose the story gives a way that is as good and as colourful as any other, for the origin is lost in the centuries which have passed.

That they have a long history is indisputable, for in very nearly every old drawing, print or painting of scene of London's riverside can be seen barges or wherries and somewhere, if one knows how to recognise them, these little peter boats. They can be seen being sailed or rowed and sometimes with the fisherman hauling in or laying out a net.

It may come as a surprise to many people that the Thames, where it runs through Westminster and the City, was ever a source of revenue for fishermen, especially if one stands on any of the bridges and looks into the murky water and at the mass of debris floating on the surface; but it must

Opposite: The Science Museum model of the 'below bridges' type of peter boat. (Photograph by courtesy of Martin Treadway)

Three views of the Author's model of an 'above bridges' type peter boat of about 1800. The scale is 1/4" = 1'0". (Photographs by courtesy of John Bowen and the Author)

be remembered that only within the last century or so London became the sprawling mass and manufacturing centre it now is.

Until 1750 there was but one bridge and so the Thames was a highway to the east or west for travellers wishing to avoid the congestion of the traffic in the narrow streets, and for those desiring to pass from the north bank to the south bank. Furthermore, the water was virtually uncontaminated; there were few factories discharging their noxious products into the stream, the disposal of sewage was of a primitive character and in any case the population as late as 1800 was certainly not above 85 000.

The river being unconfined by great stone embankments ebbed and flowed more slowly than today and so kept the water clear. Salmon were fished as far as Boulter's Lock, in fact on a memorable day in 1749 one peter boat caught thirty-five large salmon, and another one twenty-two. Other fish such as roach, plaice, shad, whitebait and eels, besides many other species, could also be caught.

There were evidently two types of peter boats: those that fished above

bridge, that is London Bridge or thereabouts in the calmer waters of the river; and those that fished in the estuary. The former were quite small clinker built boats about 18′0″ long and may be designated as the true peter boat, for they were double-ended, being exactly alike at bow and stern. The purpose of this was to allow the boat to be rowed forwards or backwards with equal facility, and in several etchings the method of fishing can also be seen.

One man, or sometimes two men, composed the crew and while one man manoeuvred the boat the other worked the net. In a painting by Samuel Scott a peter boat is seen hauling its net; the net is buoyed with corks along its upper edge and has already described a semi-circle, the rower is standing in the stern sheets rowing backwards to complete the circle and to enclose the catch. In another drawing a peterman is preparing to cast his net, which in this case is of a circular form and kept in shape by a large ring; cords from the ring lead to the end of a pole which the man is holding out from the stern of the boat.

In the estuary a larger type was used which, though described on a con-

Accurate information about peter boats is difficult to come by. However help can be found from some unexpected sources. For example, **above:** *this engraving by E W Cooke of peter boats at Greenwich will furnish the details for the interiors of these craft. (Photograph by courtesy of the Science Museum)*
Opposite: *While purists might object to this vessel being described as a peter boat, nevertheless it is one of the very few plans of these craft in existence (drawn about 1800). (Photograph by courtesy of the National Maritime Museum)*

Contemporary paintings cannot be ignored by anyone researching for a model. This painting of 'the Thames near Greenwich' by Sebastian Pether (1790 to 1884) would provide information for anyone building a diorama to display his model, but it also provides details of the craft themselves — a peter boat in the foreground. (Photograph by courtesy of the Sunderland Museum and Art Gallery)

Another type that is very similar to the peter boat is the Medway doble. This is a plan of the doble 'Louise,' drawn in 1933 when there were still seventeen of these vessels on the Medway.

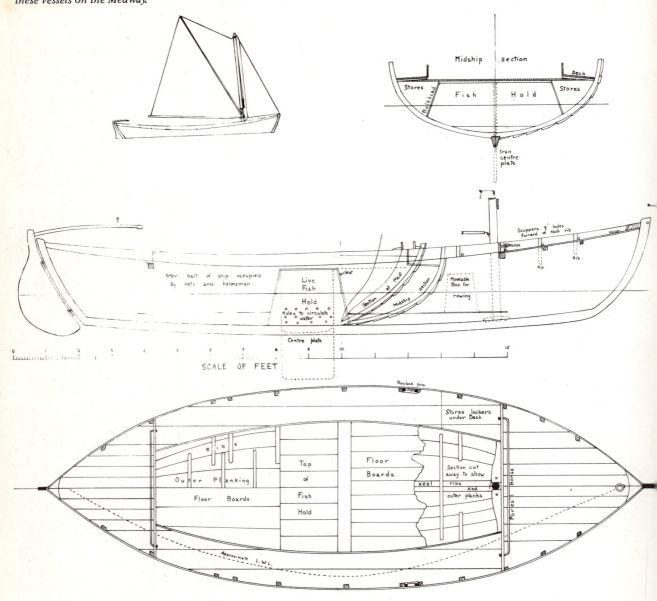

temporary draught of 1800 as "a peter boat built at Strood and noted for her superior sailing", is extremely like the present day Thames bawley or Leigh cockler. The purist would say this is not a true peter boat, so it appears as if the name came to be applied eventually to any small Thames fishing boat having a wet well.

This was an ingenious contrivance of which it is said the peter boats were the originators. In the days before refrigeration practically all perishable foods had to be preserved either by salting or drying, fish being noted especially for its lack of keeping qualities. However the peterman overcame this difficulty by building into the hull amidships a watertight compartment about 1'6" to 2'0" wide athwart the hull. Holes, about 1" in diameter, were bored through the hull sides at this position and so water from the river was admitted to the well. As the fish were caught they were placed in the well and thus were brought fresh to market or kept alive until required, which inclines one to think that Londoners of those days ate their fish fresher than we of the twentieth century.

The smaller peter boats were rowed either in a standing position or by sitting on a box placed where necessary since no thwarts were built into the boat. A sail was sometimes set on a sprit after the manner of their big brother the Thames barge, but the mast was without shrouds. The estuary type set a loose-footed gaff mainsail with topsail and foresail on a bowsprit like the bawley which it so closely resembled.

Both types had a small deck at bow and stern with a narrow length of decking connecting the two and running just below the gunwale. The drawing shows the lines of a peter boat and though not authentic can be considered as being very like the originals for no contemporary draught of the above bridges type has been preserved. But if compared with the etching by E B Cooke of peter boats at Greenwich, which clearly shows the wet wells, the build and the rig, the similarity is quite evident.

A final comparison between the two types of peter boat: the 'above bridges' boat (left) and the estuary or 'below bridges' version. (Photographs by courtesy of Martin Treadway)

CHAPTER 9

Thames wherries

The river bus for a journey from Westminster to Greenwich is but a pale shadow of the extent to which the river Thames was used before the early 1800s; for until the advent of better roads and stage coaches the river was the main highway of London and the counties each side of it. It is said that at the close of the sixteenth century 40 000 people gained their livings from the river between Windsor and Gravesend, and though this may be an exaggeration, it is nevertheless true that in Pepys' time of the second half of the seventeenth century there were 10 000 licensed watermen plying for hire.

Going by water lasted for nearly a century after Pepys' death in 1704 and the watermen drove a thriving trade, for they were protected in many different ways; for instance, the dimensions of their wherries were regulated by statute, their fares controlled as early as 1514 by Henry VIII, and they formed themselves into a company in 1555. In contrast to this the number of licensed hackney coaches in 1710 was fixed at 800 only, so instead of being bumped over streets irregularly paved with stone, passengers preferred the relatively smooth ride on the river in a craft that was cushioned, by boatmen who were sometimes notorious for their rough manners and strong language; but there was always the exception, as Dibden has sung:

>   And did you not hear of a jolly young waterman,
>   Who at Blackfriars bridge used for to ply?
>   He feather'd his oars with such skill and dexterity,
>   Winning each heart, and delighting each eye.

But what is more significant is the fact that until 1750 only one bridge, London Bridge, spanned the Thames for the use of wheeled or pedestrian traffic, so that paintings and etchings to be seen of the river as it was in the sixteenth to eighteenth centuries are not the exaggerations of contemporary

Opposite: A typical example of a present day Thames waterman's boat. (Photograph by courtesy of Arthur Pollard).

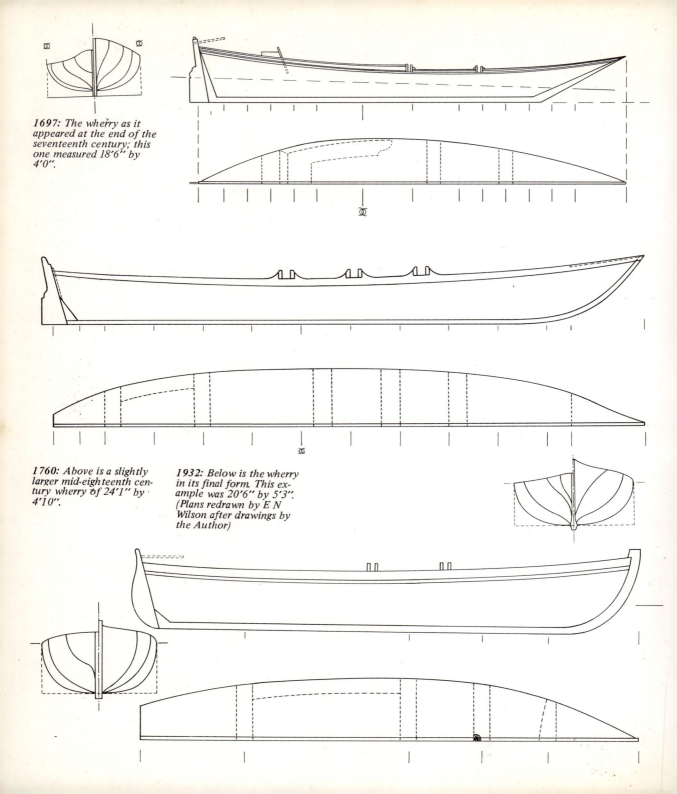

1697: The wherry as it appeared at the end of the seventeenth century; this one measured 18'6" by 4'0".

1760: Above is a slightly larger mid-eighteenth century wherry of 24'1" by 4'10".

1932: Below is the wherry in its final form. This example was 20'6" by 5'3". (Plans redrawn by E N Wilson after drawings by the Author)

artists or pure imagination, for diarists of the day all speak of the numbers of vessels of all sorts using it and of the crowded state of the river. So except by this bridge there was only one other way to cross the river and that was by a waterman's boat, or if one travelled by coach or cart, by the horse ferry on the site of present day Lambeth Bridge.

The river must have presented a very different spectacle from its present day appearance for there were no embankments and the city was soon left behind, to be succeeded by pleasant fields and market gardens stretching right down to the water's edge. Where the river passed under London Bridge, its passage was constricted by the buttresses and the water poured through at a terrifying pace, and from the bridge a writer says, in 1697, "citizens drank their genuine old port and sherry, drawn from the casks, and viewed the bridge shooters and boat races".

Prior to their passenger trade being ruined both by the bridges which were built as London expanded, and by the new forms of locomotion which became prevalent as roads were improved, the watermen were supreme—not only for passengers seeking to cross the river, but also for passage up and down the river, as well as for the loading and unloading of large vessels

This E W Cooke engraving is again a fruitful source of information about the variations in these craft. (Photograph by courtesy of the Science Museum)

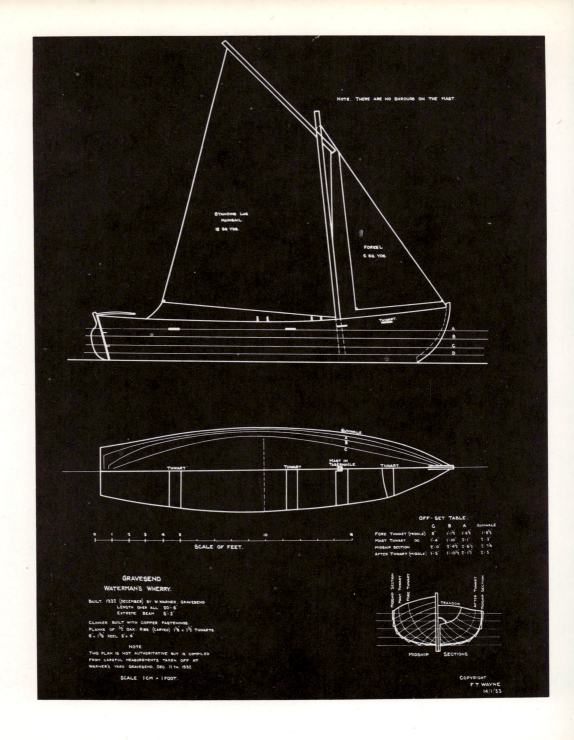

and barges bringing into the metropolis food and goods for sale and for export to other parts.

Watermen in the eighteenth century were required to serve a seven years apprenticeship and severe penalties were enforced on anyone caught breaking this rule. It would have cost you 2 pence to cross the river in a scull or 4 pence in an oared wherry, but the watermen went long distances and can be compared in this respect with the modern taxi drivers, for they plied for hire between Gravesend and Windsor, the fares in 1770 being: from London to Hammersmith 2 shillings and 6 pence; to Hampton Court 6 shillings; to Windsor 14 shillings, or to Gravesend 4 shillings and 6 pence. The watermen plied for hire from specified places called stairs, which name still survives at certain points along the river bank, where there were flights of stone steps leading down to the water where the boats lay.

The craft were light, clinker built boats very similar in appearance to those rowing boats to be seen for hire on the Serpentine in Hyde Park, or at Richmond during the summer months, and in many other places. According to contemporary sources they were built of wainscot oak, that is, the the best oak without knots or blemishes and about 1/2" thick depending on the size of the boat. Their size ranged from quite small craft up to much larger vessels, from small sculls, for one or two passengers to a wherry for a pleasure party such as Pepys often describes, up to barges of 40'0" or more which can be seen being rowed in many contemporary pictures. These were similar to, but not so ornate as, the State Barges or those owned by the various Guilds, of which the Queens Shallop of 1688 in the National Maritime Museum, Greenwich and the Charles II barge in the Royal Naval Museum in Portsmouth dockyard, are splendid examples.

The first drawing, copied from a contemporary draught, shows the lines of a wherry of 1697 and illustrates the typical extended stem, the purpose of which was to allow the bow to project over dry land, while the boat remained afloat, for the convenience of a fare being taken aboard if there were no stairs. At least that is what I have been given to understand, for it is certain that wherries of later date do not feature such a marked extension of the stem. This is quite a small boat, only 18'6" long, and, as can be seen, is of a very shallow construction; note that the waterline is not parallel with the keel and therefore it draws more water aft than at the bow. One would imagine that such a boat is suitable just for calm waters and short journeys and of course is capable of carrying only one or two passengers. Though not shown on the draught there would be seven strakes to the hull, bottom boards would have been fitted and the timbers, spaced at intervals of not more than 12", would measure 1" by 3/4". The stern sheets would have a grating or be planked just below the level of the gunwale. It would have a varnished finish, but the top strake would be painted in some bright colour such as blue or red, of the waterman's choice, and the back

The sail plan for the Gravesend wherry of 1932.

board would be decorated to match, with the owner's name and licence number shown as well.

The second drawing shows a larger wherry of 1760 which is 24'1" long and is for three pairs of oars. While possessing the hollow bow and stern of the earlier boat, as in fact do even later boats shown on draughts of 1806/1809, it does not have such an extreme bow extension. In this boat the waterline is parallel to the keel and furthermore it has a very small transom. There would be seven strakes each side together with one thicker gunwale strake each side carrying the oarlocks; the timbers would be 1" by 3/4" spaced 12" apart. Bottom boards would be laid and in the bow, level with the gunwale, there would be either a platform made up of planks or a grating. The finish would be similar to the previous example; that is, a varnished hull with a painted top strake. As regards the interior finish, generally it was normal practice for bottom boards, thwarts, gratings (in fact any part where an occupant would stand or sit) to be left in the natural state; the reason being that there would be less likelihood of the feet slipping on an unpainted surface.

As more bridges were built and roads improved so that other means of travelling became possible, the trade of the licensed watermen as a passenger service gradually died out except for the rare ferryman, such as the one at Twickenham, who was operating in 1962. Therefore the watermen have transferred their activities from occasional passenger ferrying service to general attendance on, and carrying of, small stores to ships, the safe mooring of vessels, and acting as helmsmen under the supervision of a pilot. But during the intervening decades, when sailing ships dropped anchor off Gravesend, there were passengers to be taken aboard or ashore and business to be undertaken on the ship's account, whilst their skills and expert knowledge in matters appertaining to the Thames, gained from a seven years apprenticeship, gave them that extraordinary skill so necessary when warping ships in and out of dock, or acting as pilots.

The third drawing shows a type of Gravesend waterman's wherry which

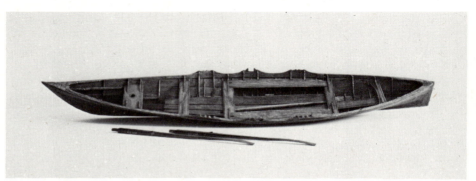

The Science Museum model of a Thames wherry. (Photograph by courtesy of Martin Treadway).

has almost disappeared from the Thames scene. It is noticeable that this boat is of a very much heavier build than the previous examples even though it is only 20'6" long. The keel is 5" deep and 4" thick, and the eight strakes of 1/2" oak are nailed to sawn timbers 1 1/8" sided by 1 1/2" moulded spaced at 1'3" intervals, and the thwarts are 8" wide by 1 3/8" thick, which all adds up to a stronger construction. The finish of these boats could be varnished or black lead, with the top strake in a contrasting colour to make identification easier, or the hull could be painted white instead of being varnished, it being all a matter of taste, but the rubbing strake was left in the natural state or treated with boiled oil. Provision is also made for setting a loose-footed lug sail, augmented on occasions with a small foresail and perhaps an even smaller mizen, for the boats ranged far below Gravesend to meet incoming vessels.

There the waterman displayed his skill in his ability to take a tow from a steamer coming light up the Thames by a process known as 'hooking on', which one imagines could be extremely hazardous. This is how the Daily Telegraph describes it in 1908: "A big steamer is coming up the Thames, lying on the thwarts of the waterman's boat is a long stout pole, with, at one end of it, a powerful hook with wide jaws. Made fast to the other end of the pole is a long coil of rope. The boat is pulled out into the fairway, until she almost seems in danger of being run down. The boat is kept just ahead of the place where the steamer will pass. At the last moment she is brought close under the steamer's bow, and when this is level with the row boat, the waterman's mate is seen standing forward with the hooked pole. When about half the steamer's length has passed, the man with the hook deftly places it over the steamer's bulwarks. The hooked pole holds, and then comes another exciting moment when the boatman has payed out sufficient of the rope attached to the pole. The boatman catches a turn round the forward thwart. At once the rope tautens, and with a forward jump the row boat is hauled through the water at a swishing pace. The bow rises, and her stern sinks and the sensation when the boat first shoots ahead is a shock such as a whaler's boat crew experience when they make fast to the leviathan of the deep".

Present day Thames watermen have practically discarded the use of pulling boats, even though the annual race for watermen just out of their apprenticeship—the Doggett Coat and Badge—still takes place over the course between London Bridge and Chelsea. The boats in use today are often converted ex-Admiralty harbour motor launches, either clinker built or diagonally planked and ranging up to about 36'0" in length, or specially built hard chine steel launches with a wheelhouse and fore cabin, seating being arranged aft for passengers. These craft are frequently called into service because of the new oil refineries in the lower reaches of the Thames, and for ships coming up river to the docks under the supervision of Trinity House pilots.

CHAPTER 10

Southwold beach yawls

A century and more ago, hundreds of sailing craft passed up and down the East Coast between the northern and Baltic ports, and London. They could have been passenger vessels, colliers, trading ships or fishing craft, and if southerly gales were encountered they found a natural shelter and rendezvous in the deep water channel known as Yarmouth Roads lying between Winterton in Norfolk and Southwold in Suffolk. Here they would lie up waiting until more favourable conditions allowed them to proceed, and it is here that we find the East Anglian beach yawls—open boats peculiar to this stretch of the coast, and which formed the basis for subsequent development of the lifeboats.

They were used, amongst other purposes, for the pilot service and also for the transport of stores, provisions and passengers to and from the many sailing ships anchored in the roads. Because of the variation in local conditions they were quite unlike other craft and were of an unusual size, for they were the largest type of open boat employed around the English coasts, being from 45'0" long to as much as 75'0" long, and were reputed to be the fastest undecked boats in existence. According to Dixon Kemp, in *Yachts and Boat Sailing*, 1891, they regularly attained speeds of 13, 14 or even 15 knots.

In hull form the yawls were remarkably like the Norse longships, but with less sheer and with the stem and sternpost set almost vertically. For their size they were of very light construction and were double-ended, clinker built of oak, and manned by eight to fourteen pairs of oars. The earlier yawls carried three lug sails but the general practice later became for them to be fitted with only two loose-footed lug sails of larger size. The foresail, lashed to an iron hook extending from the stemhead, was a dipping lug

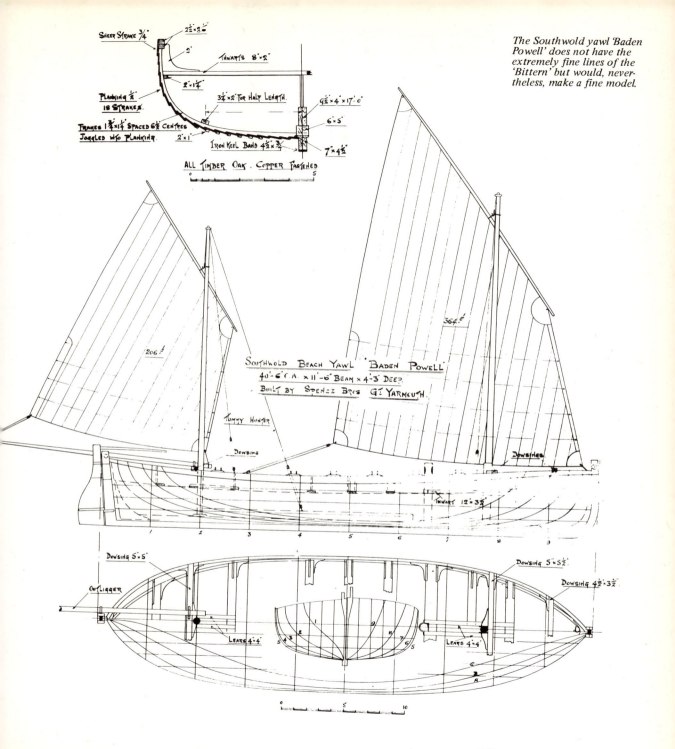

The Southwold yawl 'Baden Powell' does not have the extremely fine lines of the 'Bittern' but would, nevertheless, make a fine model.

which had to be lowered and set again on the other side of the mast whenever the vessel went about. The mizen was a standing lug sail spread by a very long outrigger extending from the stern.

Some years ago I went to Southwold and saw in the fishermen's club house on the cliff top a fairly large model about 3'0" long of a beach yawl which attracted my attention and of which I made a number of sketches. I was delighted, therefore, to find in the Science Museum at that time a print of a draught of this particular boat, the *Bittern,* built in 1892. It has a table of offsets and a specification so that with the few minor details of the rigging which I have appended, it is possible to build an authentic model of a type of craft which has now entirely disappeared; if this is done to a scale of say 1/12 or 1/24, it could be built exactly like the original. My model was to a scale of 1/4" = 1'0" (1/48) and gives an excellent idea of the appearance. The brief details which I have added below will be useful, as well as pointing out certain peculiarities.

There should be two thwart clamps, 1 1/2" by 2" wide, to support the ends of the thwarts; these extend to just beyond the fore and aft thwarts. It is worth noting that some of the thwarts have lodging knees but all have two knees at each end, the forward one of which reaches to the top of the washboard, the other after one only to the gunwale. The bilge stringers are the same size as the thwart clamps and reach to the gratings. On each side of the keelson, up to the bilge stringers, bottom boards are laid on battens,

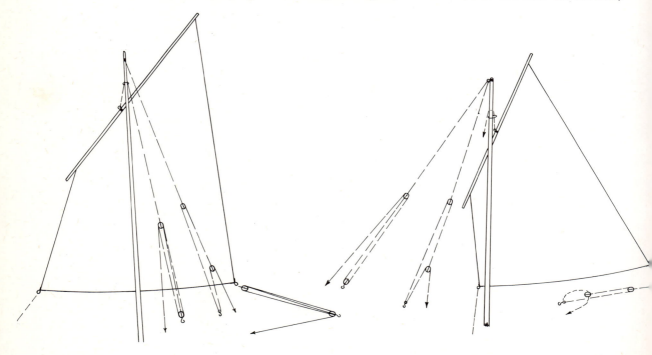

The Author's model of 'Bittern' won a Silver Medal at a recent Model Engineer Exhibition. (Photograph by courtesy of the Author)

and there is a total of eight boards amidships. The gratings in the bow and stern just cover the ends of the floor boards and are a little above them. The samson post, about 6" square, is secured by an iron strap to the fourth thwart and rests on the keelson. The masts are stepped in sockets on the keelson and are supported by a thwart resting on the clamp and above this, just below the top of the washboard, by a square thwart on which is a cleat to which the masts are held by iron straps; the forward strap is hinged on the port side, and the after strap is hinged on the starboard side. An iron band, 1" thick, is fastened to the stem and passes along the keel and up the sternpost, and there is another one round the bow on the gunwale just below the iron hook attached to the stem head. Poppets, to fit in the oarlocks, are secured by cords to the thwart clamp.

The boat is painted white inside and outside, except for the thwarts, bottom boards and gratings, but the outside of the washboard is painted in a contrasting colour which could be blue, red or green and on this, at the bow, is the name *Bittern* and at the stern the owner's name and port *H. Hurr Southwold*.

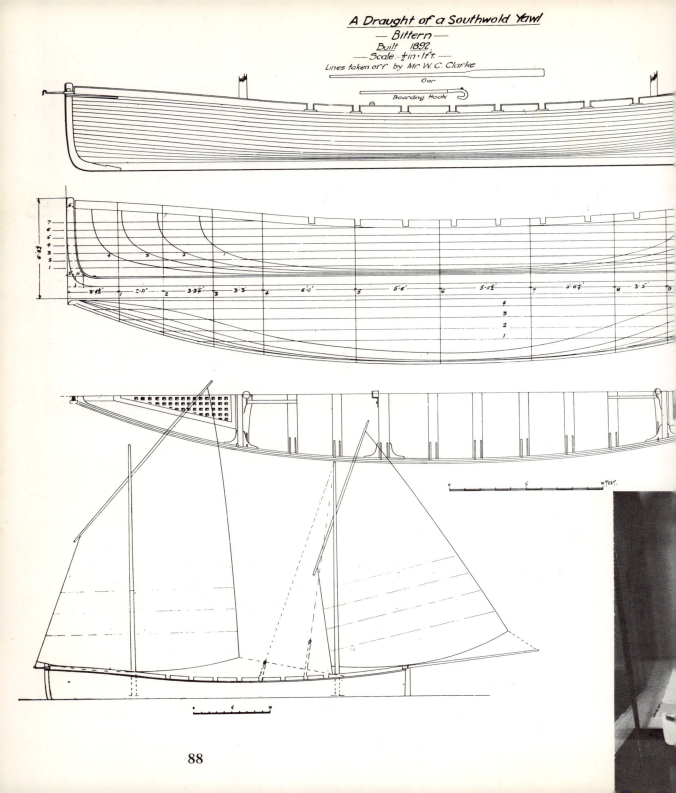

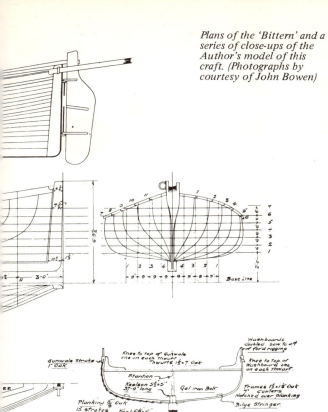

Plans of the 'Bittern' and a series of close-ups of the Author's model of this craft. (Photographs by courtesy of John Bowen)

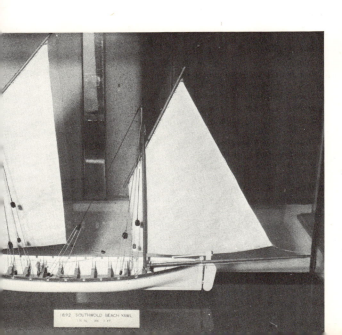

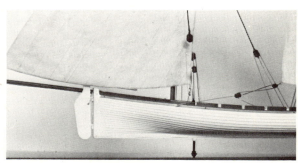

The dimensions of the spars are: fore mast 34'0" long, 8" diameter; fore yard 28'0" long; mizen mast 31'0" long, 8" diameter; mizen yard 22'0" long; outrigger, set to port through an iron ring at the head of the sternpost, 26'6" long, of which 17'6" is outboard.

The tackle to support the masts is belayed to eyes or cleats fitted on the inside of the gunwale; I have indicated the approximate positions of these on the draught. H is where the tackle is hooked to an eye and C is where the fall is belayed to a cleat; also on the keelson, aft of the samson post, is an eye for the mizen stay.

The dimensions of the sails can be taken off the draught, noting the lines of the reef points and that the bolt ropes are on the port side. On each yard is an iron band with an eye into which is hooked the end of the halliard, which then passes through an iron ring around the mast, through a sheave in the masthead and down to a two part tackle. The shrouds and stays are secured by shackles to eyes on an iron band at the masthead; the separate sketches show how the sails and masts are rigged.

Research will reveal many more interesting types of open boats that are suitable prototypes for modelling, such as this contemporary waterman's boat. (Photograph by courtesy of Arthur Pollard)

Glossary

The bearding line is the line to which the rabbet on the stem, keel and sternpost is cut for the planking.
Benches are the seats placed in the stern-sheets on which the passengers sit.
The bilge is that part of the hull which, if lying unsupported, touches the ground.
A bilge keel is a false keel fixed along the line of the bilges for their protection.
Bottom boards are planks laid fore and aft or athwartships for the protection of the interior of the bottom of the boat.
The bow is the fore end of a vessel.
A breast hook is a shaped bracket secured in the bows to brace the sides of the hull to the stem.
Carlings are pieces of wood fastened fore and aft between the deck beams.
A carvel built hull is smooth sided, the planks being laid edge to edge.
The ceiling is the inside skin of the hull between the keelson and the gunwale. Also called the foot-walings.
A centreboard is a board which can be lowered through the keel to avoid leeway and give greater stability.
A clinker, clincher, or clench built hull is one in which each upper plank overlaps the lower one.
The crosshead is a bar fixed athwartships at the rudder head to which ropes are attached for steering.
Deadwoods are shaped pieces of wood fixed in the angle between the joints of the keel and stem, and the keel and sternpost.
A double-ended boat is pointed at both ends enabling it to be rowed with facility either forwards or backwards.
Foot-walings See *ceiling*.
Forefoot is the intersection of the stem and keel.
Frames are sawn or built up shaped timbers fixed to the keel onto which the planks of the hull are secured.
The garboard strake is the plank fixed nearest to the keel.
A grating is a wooden platform in which the holes are square.
The grip is the handle of the oar.
The gudgeon is the tube part of the rudder hinge in which the pintle works.
The gunwale is the thick strip of wood fastened over, or onto, the top strake to strengthen it, and to which fittings are attached.

A hog is a plank of wood laid over the keel to which it secures the garboard strakes and prevents transverse movement.
Hooded ends are the ends of the planks where they are rabbeted together and also into the stem or stern.
The keel is the longitudinal backbone to which the stem and stern are fixed.
Knees are shaped brackets of wood or metal to secure the ends of the thwarts to the hull.
Lapstrake is the plank of a clinker built boat.
Lapstreak means the same as clinker built.
Loom is the shaft of the oar.
An oar is the long, shaped piece of wood by means of which the boat is propelled through the water.
Oarports are holes in the hull through which the oars are passed from outboard and used instead of rowlocks.
The paddle is the wide part of the oar which dips into the water; also a very short oar.
The painter is a rope attached to the stem and used for towing the boat.
The pintle is the pin of the rudder hinge.
Planks are the strips of wood used to build up the hull and which are rabbeted into the stem and sternpost.
Rabbets are the grooves in the stem and sternpost into which the ends of the planks are fastened.
Ribs are another name for the frames or timbers.
A rower is a man who pulls on the oar.
Rowlocks are semi-circular metal hooks, tenoned into the gunwales and into which the oars are placed when rowing.
The rubber or rubbing strake is a strip of wood fixed about the level of the gunwales to protect the planks from damage.
The rudder is a shaped piece of wood hinged to the stern and moved by the tiller in order to steer the boat.
Scantling is the transverse dimensions of a piece of timber.
Sheer is the curve formed by the gunwale.
The sheer strake is the top strake of a hull.
The stem is the fore vertical extension of the keel.
The stern is the after end of a vessel.
The sternpost is the aft vertical extension of the keel onto which the transom is fastened.
Sternsheets are that part of the boat between the stern and the after thwart; the place for passengers.
Strakes are the planks forming the sides of the hull and which are rabbetted into the stem and sternpost.
A stretcher is a bar or plank of wood placed athwartships at the rower's feet as an aid to rowing.
A stringer is a longitudinal strip of wood laid over the timbers to strengthen them or to act as supports for the thwarts.
Thole pins are wooden pins tenoned into the gunwales as an alternative to rowlocks.
Thwarts are the seats on which the rowers sit.
The thwart clamp is the stringer supporting the ends of the thwarts.
Thwart pillars are turned supports placed centrally under the thwarts and which rest on the keelson.
The tiller is the bar acting as a lever to turn the rudder, usually removeable when unshipping the rudder.
Timbers are the ribs or frames supporting the sides of the hull. They are either sawn to shape or bent into position.
The trunk is the watertight box in which the centreboard is pivoted.
The transom is the stern of the boat, fitted square across the sternpost.

Further research

SOME USEFUL BOOKS
Boat Building, Howard Chapelle, 1941.
American Small Sailing Craft, Howard Chapelle, 1951.
The National Watercraft Collection, Howard Chapelle, 1960.
Architectura Navalis Mercatoria, F-H af Chapman, 1768, (reprinted 1971).
Sketches of Shipping and Craft, E W Cooke, 1829.
The Practice of Shipbuilding, John Fincham, 1812.
The Sailing Boat, H C Folkard, 1863, (reprinted 1973).
Water Transport, J Hornell, 1946.
A Manual of Yacht and Boat Sailing, Dixon Kemp, 1891.
Sailing Drifters, Edgar March, 1953.
Sailing Trawlers, Edgar March, 1954.
Inshore Craft of Britain in the Days of Sail and Oar, Edgar March, 2 vols, 1970.
Clenched Lap or Clinker, Eric McKee, 1972.
The Last Days of Mast and Sail, Sir Alan Moore, 1925, (reprinted 1970).
Mast and Sail in Europe and Asia, Warrington Smyth, 1906.
Yachting Monthly. A series of articles on small craft published between 1933 and 1938, included: a beach yawl (April 1933); Sheringham crab boats (September 1933); Lowestoft shrimping boats (October 1933); Yorkshire cobles (December 1933); and an Aldeburgh sprat boat (January 1934).

OPEN BOAT MODELS

Most maritime museums in this country contain models of undecked vessels, but models of the specific types mentioned in this book can be found in the following places.

The Science Museum, London, houses the finest collection of small craft in Britain. All the craft dealt with in this book are represented except the Lowestoft shrimper.

Great Yarmouth Museum has a model of a Sheringham crabber and a model provisionally identified as a peter boat.

Gray Art Gallery and Museum, Hartlepool, has half-models of a Yorkshire and a Northumberland coble, and two full models of the latter type.

Hull Maritime Museum has a number of coble models in its collection, including Filey and Flamborough fishing cobles and a half-model of a Northumberland type.

Whitby Museum also contains models of a wide range of cobles, including a pilot coble and a powered version.

The Trawl public house in Grimsby is the home for most of the Author's original models discussed in this book. They are on permanent display—during opening hours of course!

The Author's model of the Aldeburgh sprat boat. (Photograph by courtesy of the Author)
Overleaf: *The real thing at work — unloading sprats in Lowestoft harbour. (Photograph by courtesy of the Port of Lowestoft Research Society)*